T
ROMA

MARK RICHARDS

Shepherd's Walks

Published in 2006 by Shepherd's Walks
Kirkharle Courtyard, Kirkwhelpington, Northumberland NE19 2PE

Copyright © Mark Richards 2006

ISBN 0 9552624 0 2 | 978 0 9552624 0 1

Printed by Carnmor Print & Design, 95-97 London Road, PRESTON Lancashire PR1 4BA

*While every care has been taken to ensure the information in this guide is correct
going to press, please bear in mind that over time changes will inevitably occur.
The author welcomes feedback from walkers to ensure that future editions are reliable:
your confidence and enjoyment are paramount.*

— ACKNOWLEDGEMENTS —
THE AUTHOR WISHES TO RECORD HIS GRATEFUL THANKS TO THE
FOLLOWING INDIVIDUALS FOR THEIR CONSTRUCTIVE ADVICE & ENCOURAGEMENT:

PAUL BENIAMS HERITAGE & WILDLIFE GUIDE; KATHARINE BIRDSALL NORTH PENNINES AONB;
ANDREW BIRLEY THE VINDOLANDA TRUST; DAVID CADWGAN FRIENDS OF HALTWHISTLE RINGS;
JOHN CLARKE FEATHERSTONE CASTLE; COLIN EARNSHAW MID TYNE COMMUNITY TRUST;
TIM FISH NORTHUMBERLAND COUNTY COUNCIL; CLAIRE FURNESS NATURAL ENGLAND;
PHIL GRAY EAST CUMBRIA COUNTRYSIDE PROJECT; LIZ KELLY HALTWHISTLE PARTNERSHIP;
PAGET & LORNA LAZZARI NORTHUMBERLAND NATIONAL PARK AUTHORITY;
PETER MOGRIDGE TYNEDALE RURAL TRANSPORT PARTNERSHIP OFFICER;
DAVID McGLADE HADRIAN'S WALL PATH NATIONAL TRAIL OFFICER; RACHEL NEWMAN OXFORD
ARCHAEOLOGY NORTH; RICHARD NEWMAN CUMBRIA COUNTY COUNCIL; ANDREW NICHOLSON
EAST CUMBRIA COUNTRYSIDE PROJECT; DAVID O'HARA RSPB; GEORGINA PLOWRIGHT ENGLISH
HERITAGE; ANDREW POAD THE NATIONAL TRUST; MARTIN SHAW NATURAL ENGLAND;
FIONA WATSON THE VINDOLANDA TRUST; SIMON WILSON NORTH PENNINES AONB;
DUNCAN WISE NORTHUMBERLAND NATIONAL PARK AUTHORITY.

WITH A SPECIAL MENTION FOR NICK LEEMING WHO GENEROUSLY PROOF READ THE GUIDE
AND MY WIFE HELEN WHO HAS LIVED WITH THIS BOOK FROM THE SPARK OF AN IDEA!

HADRIAN'S WALL
CONSERVATION CORRIDOR

DEDICATED TO JOHN CLAYTON
OF CHESTERS HOUSE, CHOLLERFORD.

JOHN CLAYTON HOLDS A UNIQUE AND HONOURED PLACE AS A MODERN
HERO OF THE WALL. HIS FORESIGHT, AND FOR THE LAST FORTY YEARS OF
HIS LIFE, PASSION TO PRESERVE WHAT WAS LEFT OF HADRIAN'S WALL IN
THE VICTORIAN AGE, MADE HIM PRE-EMINENT AS A FOUNDER OF THE
CONSERVATION MOVEMENT. WITHOUT HIS ACQUISITION OF FARMS ALONG
THE WHIN SILL THERE WOULD BE PRECIOUS LITTLE OF THE MONUMENT LEFT
FOR THE PUBLIC TO SEE AND DRAW HERITAGE INSPIRATION FROM TODAY.

CONTENTS

FOREWORD

I AM PASSIONATE ABOUT HERITAGE,
AND SHARING IT. HADRIAN'S WALL IS FANTASTIC,
AND WE CAN BENEFIT A LOT MORE FROM IT.

MARK RICHARDS' NEW BOOK PROVIDES A
WONDERFUL EXPLORATION OF THE HADRIAN'S
WALL LANDSCAPE, GIVING THE READER,
AND OF COURSE, THE WALKER,
A CHANCE TO SEE IT FROM
A DIFFERENT PERSPECTIVE.

LEISURE AND TOURISM ARE KEY TO
THE ECONOMY OF THE WALL CORRIDOR.

THIS HELPFUL BOOK OPENS UP MORE
OPPORTUNITIES FOR WALKERS,
WHATEVER THE WEATHER,
WHATEVER THE SEASON,
AND IS JUST THE SORT OF 'ENTERPRISE'
THAT HADRIAN'S WALL HERITAGE
WANTS TO ENCOURAGE.

ANN GREEN
CHAIRMAN OF
HADRIAN'S WALL HERITAGE LIMITED

The Blood Stone on Cragend looking to Greenlee Lough

EXPLORE THE WALL IN THE ROUND

The Hadrian's Wall frontier was as deep as it was broad. During the garrison's life, foot and cavalry patrols headed north and south to quell Caledonian, and native British uprisings, keeping order between outpost forts. Yet walkers on the National Trail know this historic setting only from the narrow, largely remote perspective, of the actual mural line, their only solace - the boast that they have walked the Wall. No wonder they get sucked into break-neck schedules blinkered to the achievement of a six-day coast to coast walking challenge.

The Roman Ring has been devised to bring a more relaxed vision of precisely what walking through Roman Wall Country is all about. The book is intended to open visitors' eyes to the diversity and richness of the greater landscape, allied to Hadrian's Wall World Heritage Site, and to highlight the long history of man's activities in this fascinating border country. Leave your car at home. Come to Hadrian's Wall unshackled and carfree. Incorporate a string of fascinating valley-based service-centre communities, and year-round public transport facilities, including six railway stations, into expedition planning. Instead of restricting yourself to a ruthless schedule, consider devoting several long weekends, over a period of time, to discovering different aspects of the frontier.

In 1992, exploring Hadrian's Wall from coast to coast, I garnered material, and subsequently handcrafted as an illustrated walking guide in pen & ink. 'The Wall Walk' was published the following year by Cicerone Press, a year later I delved into the hinterland for 'Wall Country Walks'. Preparing these books gave me the 'big picture' of Roman Wall Country. My experience with Offa's Dyke Path had made me keenly aware of the sensitive issues involved in creating a regular pathway so close to, and frequently directly upon, vulnerable archaeology. With no tourism publicity my Hadrian's Wall guides sold quietly, reaching only a small historically-conscious audience.

A full decade was to pass before the inauguration of Hadrian's Wall Path, a period during which the wisdom of formalising a National Trail, precisely upon so sensitive an archaeological relic was hotly debated. Hence in May 2003 it might be said that archaeological caution was swept aside by economic enthusiasm. The notion of walking coast to coast along such a treasured historic monument has proved irresistible to a broad spectrum of society, from home and abroad. Hence the establishment of the Hadrian's Wall Path, as an official National Trail, within the Roman frontier World Heritage Site, has brought pleasure to an amazing number of people.

However, success can be a double-edged sword: thousands of boots, pounding the pastures at the foot of the Wall, have eroded the Path in many places. No wonder that those charged with the care of the World Heritage Site, have instituted the popular Summer Passport scheme, and have sought to discourage winter walking when surface damage to the National Trail is at its greatest. The best interests of sustainable management must always prevail: we should treasure this frontier, not beat it to death. Anyone who has seen my 'Wall Walk' guide will have noticed the cruelly eroded path on Cuddy's Crags gracing the cover, today it has been re-routed and melded by pitching (witness below).

HADRIAN'S WALL CONSERVATION CORRIDOR

While there is but one path focused directly upon the most sensitive archaeology, a dilemma will remain. Why hasn't the Roman Military Way been formalised as the wet weather route?

Housesteads Crags from Cuddy's Crags

Unfortunately, the 'official guide' does not alleviate the stress on the main path by describing this one route, in one direction. Hence the impetuous behind the proposal in this guide: designate the central sector as the 'Hadrian's Wall Conservation Corridor'. Not a stuffy form of words, but an inspirational call to all who wish to explore this great frontier landscape on foot. Enabling them to play their part in sustaining both the Trail's harmony with the monument, and support the local economy.

The World Heritage Site designation identifies the linear Roman frontier in archaeological terms. The Conservation Corridor is a broad framework of paths, extending awareness of the diverse qualities of this famous landscape for leisured walks. The corridor focuses on that part of the National Trail in contact with the most sensitive archaeology, principally along the Whin Sill, but including important connected stretches of the monument to east and west. Of greater significance is the countryside to north and south of the Wall: the raison d'etre for this guide.

To more clearly define the corridor two new linear paths have been identified, The Roman Ring and the Moss Troopers' Trail, running south and north of the Wall respectively, with several north/south

Native woodland at the heart of glorious Geltsdale

routes and branches

HADRIAN'S WALL PATH
within Hadrian's Wall Conservation Corridor
53 km | **33** miles > **3** days

MOSS TROOPERS' TRAIL
Carvoran to Newbrough
32 km | **20** miles > **2** days

Northumberland
National Park

SIMONBURN

NEWBROUGH

FOURSTONES

GILSLAND

CORBRIDGE

GREENHEAD

HALTWHISTLE   BARDON   HAYDON   HEXHAM
MILL   BRIDGE

BRAMPTON

HALLBANKGATE

TALKIN   COLD FELL

*North Pennines Area of
Outstanding Natural Beauty*

THE ROMAN RING
Haytongate to Halton Chesters
83 km | **52** miles > **4** days

links, and even a real mountain, added for spice! The Roman Ring is the linchpin of the whole structure: a fascinating exposé, roughly parallel to, and south of the Wall, connecting at either end with the National Trail. More than a winter's trail, rather it is a path for all seasons, and the basis of a variety of circular expeditions.

This book allows you the flexibility to devise your own roaming ring route with either the National Trail; the Moss Troopers' Trail, which takes a swipe into the wilder country immediately north of the Whin Sill, or by incorporating one or more of the link paths. The Roman Ring with Hadrian's Wall Path produces a long walk, equal in length to the National Trail, for most walkers this will be the dream ticket to savour in a seven-day trip.

As presently instituted, The Roman Ring is an unofficial route and therefore carries no distinguishing waymarks. Standards of path maintenance are coincident with the general state of rural path care, fortunately in this area these standards are high and walkers should have few moments of navigational doubt. The route is described from an eastbound perspective (anti-clockwise), but includes a westbound (clockwise) description too, because in common with

Regular 94 bus waiting at Hallbankgate

the National Trail the walker may travel in either direction. Where one begins is a personal matter. The route is described from the precise points of divergence from the National Trail, but guidance is given from the key intermediate rail stations and bus stops: Brampton (bus), Brampton Junction (rail), Hallbankgate (bus), Haltwhistle (rail & bus), Vindolanda (bus), Bardon Mill (rail & bus), Haydon Bridge (rail & bus), Hexham (rail & bus), Corbridge (rail & bus).

HADRIAN'S WALL PATH

The National Trail is not described in this guide, as it is the author's hope that you will acquire a copy of his current Cicerone Press guide, newly updated for 2006. The perfect companion, it describes the Wall Walk in both directions with the same attention to fascinating detail and careful guidance you may expect.

Trailworthy Awareness | ***help sustain the Wall Walk by***
FOLLOWING THE ROMAN RING, INSTEAD OF THE MID SECTION OF THE NATIONAL TRAIL FROM THE END OF OCTOBER UNTIL THE BEGINNING OF APRIL — IT'S THE GREEN WINTER'S TRAIL.

LOCAL CIRCULAR WALK LEAFLETS

Hadrian's Wall Conservation Corridor provides a super-imposed structure, in concert with the National Trail, to complement the many short circular walks described in locally-prepared leaflets (available from TICs). The annually updated leaflet 'Walking around Hadrian's Wall Country', details the current crop of circular walk leaflets available within the area. This includes the Haltwhistle Rings, Mid Tyne Walks and the Hadrian's Wall Link Path series prepared by the East Cumbria Countryside Project. The leaflet also draws attention to all important public transport facilities: Tyne Valley Line trains, plus rural and pan-Wall bus services.

HADRIAN'S WALL INFORMATION LINE 01434 322002
info@hadrians-wall.org   www.hadrians-wall.org

MAPS COVERING THE CONSERVATION CORRIDOR : LANDRANGER 86 Haltwhistle & Brampton **87** Hexham & Haltwhistle   **EXPLORER 315** Brampton, Longtown & Gretna Green **OL43** Hadrian's Wall and **HARVEY MAPS** – Hadrian's Wall Path

FOR NEWS OF THE ALL-ROUND EXPERIENCE
visit : www.theromanring.com

THE VINDOLANDA TRUST

Vindolanda provides all those engaged in The Roman Ring with the opportunity to visit one of the most exciting and interesting sites within the Hadrian's Wall World Heritage Site. The site is changing year on year as our on-going programme of archaeological excavations continues to reveal the story of Vindolanda - from the beginning of April to the end of August each year, with archaeologists working on site Sunday to Friday each week (weather permitting). The extensive remains at the site are complimented by sections of reconstructed fort wall, an open air museum and an extensive museum housing the most impressive finds form the site, a display and film about the Vindolanda Writing Tablets as well as a cafe and gift shop. Please note that the facilities at Vindolanda are only available to visitors to the site, admission can be paid at either the museum or main site entrance. As an independent charitable trust, by visiting the site you will be directly contributing to the continued excavation and development of Vindolanda. Toilets for walkers can be found adjacent to the admissions building at the main Vindolanda car park.

Carvoran is the perfect start for the Moss Troopers' Trail, as a hub of activity from Roman times when it marked a cross-roads in two major Roman transport routes. Before you start your walk, visit the Roman Army Museum, open daily from mid-February to mid-November at 10 a.m. A great introduction to Roman military life on Hadrian's Wall and featuring the superb Eagle's Eye Film, an aerial guided tour of a section of Hadrian's Wall with a virtually reconstructed return flight showing how the area may have looked almost 2000 years ago. The museum does have a car park, cafe, shop and toilets, however these are for the use of paying museum visitors, so if you are just starting out on your walk from here, please park in the Walltown Quarry car park just down the road. For more information about the Roman Army Museum and The Vindolanda Trust, visit **www.vindolanda.com**

Fiona Watson, Heritage Information Officer, The Vindolanda Trust

NORTHUMBERLAND NATIONAL PARK

Stand anywhere along the central section of Hadrian's Wall with your back to the Tyne Valley and look north across the wind-swept mires to the edge of Wark Forest; and it is clear why so many visitors' most memorable impression of the Wall is its setting. Much of the landscape in question is protected and cared for as Northumberland National Park – England's most northerly, and it covers an area of 400 sq miles from the Wall all the way to the Cheviot Hills on the Scottish Border. With just a scattering of isolated farms in sight, it is also of no surprise that it is England's most unpopulated National Park and the sense of space and tranquillity here is overwhelming.

The Moss Troopers' Trail offers views that most visitors simply do not see – the Roman Wall from the north, as it crests the defensive and vertical crags of the Whin Sill. It must indeed have been a sobering sight to the local Celts who could not escaped undeniable might of the Roman Empire in front of them. Northumberland National Park Authority looks after a number of sites along the Moss Troopers' Trail. Walltown to the west was once an industrial quarry providing road stone. It has since been transformed into an attractive country park supplying information and refreshments – ideal for picnics. Greenlee Lough on the other hand is managed for its birdlife and a boardwalk through the reed beds and public birdhide enable you to get closer to the action.

For more information on how to explore the rest of Northumberland National Park and the surrounding area, call in to our National Park Centre at Once Brewed **01434 344396**, or visit **www.northumberland-national-park.org.uk**.

Duncan Wise, Team Leader – Visitor Services, Northumberland National Park Authority

THE ROMAN RING

LANERCOST PRIORY | HALTON CHESTERS

84 km | **52.5** miles > **4** days

A PATH FOR ALL SEASONS

HAYTONGATE TO BRAMPTON JUNCTION

7 km | **4.4** miles > **2.4** hours

(1)

With the majority of walkers choosing to follow Hadrian's Wall Path westward, THE ROMAN RING falls in line, adopting an anti-clockwise progression in its principal description leading from the National Trail. In the western sector walkers either branch directly at Haytongate, en route to Lanercost Priory, or step onto the route a little further south, either at Brampton Market Place (with its regular bus services) or embark from Brampton Junction Station, where year-round train services halt upon the Newcastle to Carlisle Line. This is one of the world's first commercial railways, the Newcastle to Greenhead section opening in 1836. However, it is prudent to check the timetable carefully, as stopping trains are becoming ever more infrequent, so don't put all your chickens in this one basket... it is wise to think bus first!

1 The Roman Ring breaks south from the line of Hadrian's Wall and the National Trail at Haytongate (grid reference 554645). Situated between the invisible sites of turret 53b and milecastle 54, this is a special spot, not so much for its Roman interest rather roaming interest, being the site of a much-patronised and hugely appreciated self-service trail refreshment station. Follow the access drive downhill to merge with the bridle-lane from Walton Wood Lodge, continuing left to the public road at Lanercost.

2 To glory in the serene environs of Lanercost Priory go right, through the ruined gatehouse arch, to the parish church. The adjacent ruins are managed by English Heritage, accessed via a doorway to the right. The Priory plays a very active role in the wider local community hosting a range of concerts, craft exhibitions and flower festivals. The building is worthy of your avid attention.

MAP 1

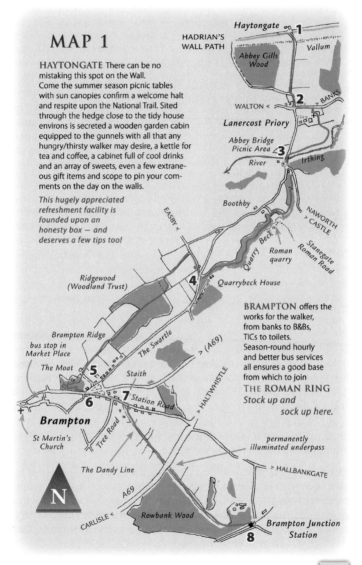

HAYTONGATE There can be no mistaking this spot on the Wall. Come the summer season picnic tables with sun canopies confirm a welcome halt and respite upon the National Trail. Sited through the hedge close to the tidy house environs is secreted a wooden garden cabin equipped to the gunnels with all that any hungry/thirsty walker may desire, a kettle for tea and coffee, a cabinet full of cool drinks and an array of sweets, even a few extraneous gift items and scope to pin your comments on the day on the walls.

This hugely appreciated refreshment facility is founded upon an honesty box — and deserves a few tips too!

HADRIAN'S WALL PATH

Haytongate **1**

Abbey Gills Wood

Vallum

WALTON < **2**

> BANKS

Lanercost Priory

Abbey Bridge Picnic Area **3**

River Irthing

Boothby

NAWORTH > CASTLE

EASBY <

Quarry Beck

Roman quarry

Stanegate Roman Road

Ridgewood (Woodland Trust)

4 *Quarrybeck House*

BRAMPTON offers the works for the walker, from banks to B&Bs, TICs to toilets. Season-round hourly and better bus services all ensures a good base from which to join THE ROMAN RING Stock up and sock up here.

Brampton Ridge bus stop in Market Place

The Swartle

> (A69)

The Moat **5**

Staith

> HALTWHISTLE

6 **7** *Station Road*

Brampton

St Martin's Church

Tree Road

permanently illuminated underpass

The Dandy Line

A69

> HALLBANKGATE

CARLISLE <

Rowbank Wood

Brampton Junction Station **8**

N

13

Lanercost Priory was founded in 1166 by Robert de Vaux for Augustinian Canons. Much its life and times are poorly recorded. However, due to illness, King Edward I and his court resided here for six months. It is strange to think that the governance of England was based here at Lanercost: a momentous event indeed!

The west range of the monastic living quarters remains intact, it was used as domestic accommodation by Sir Thomas Dacre who acquired the estate in 1536 after the Dissolution. The elegant church nave has been preserved, serving as the parish church: almost the entire elegant building is composed of solid, neatly tooled, Roman stone, brought down in cartloads from the Wall.

Alternatively, follow the roadside footway left. You will notice that the wall to the right is composed of Wall stone, reminiscent of the Clayton wall on the Whin Sill. After about 120 metres, follow the footpath right at a wooden hand-gate 'River Irthing'. Advance towards the priory church, go left through the kissing-gate, follow the gravel path in the graveyard round the east end of the ruined chancel. Pass through the kissing-gate into a small field, attention will inevitably be drawn to the ruins close at hand, within the fenced compound you may see visitors strolling intently with hand-held audio guides.

Pass by the orchard, with active areas of fruit and vegetables, akin to a monastic herbarium. Cross a stile into the large meadow, continue straight ahead to a tall white-topped wooden pointer on the old riverbank. Turn right following the river downstream, note the evidence of flood erosion eating into the near banks, at a kissing-gate emerge onto the road.

3 Go straight across the road, through the facing wicket-gate, into the picnic area with its grand rustic seats and table, a millennium project beautifully executed by Alister Neville. Turn left over the pedestrianised old bridge, take your time crossing this elegant structure, with its refuges and lovely river views. The River Irthing, long been renown as a haven for otter, drains a vast moorland catchment, hence its rich peaty turbidity. Reaching the road beside the former Abbey Bridge Hotel cross over, passing the former Abbey Mill, well-tended but no longer a working corn mill. Ascend the Naworth Castle road: be watchful as there are no verges, a footpath, signed 'Brampton via Quarrybeck' guides to the right.

After 30 metres, hand-railed steps lead down, over the dry mill-leat, to the beck-side path leading via a stout footbridge made from a tree-trunk (hand-rail). The journey upstream is a peculiar pleasure almost every step of the way, including looking down upon a charming waterfall tumbling over the red sandstone bedrock. However, there can be moments of bank erosion and wind blown trees, so be watchful (fortunately the ECCP are vigilant in this area). A metal kissing-gate heralds a brief open passage at the foot of a steep pasture bank, before regaining the woodland way at a kissing-gate. On arriving at the quarry yard, where 'Natural Stone Direct' runs a stone cutting and distribution business, it is interesting to realize that it is on the site of a Roman quarry - from which the beck-name derives. Indeed, the Stanegate, a pre-Hadrianic road, runs through the site, a rare survival of this ancient thoroughfare, which linked Carlisle (Luguvalium) with Corbridge (Corstopitum).

4 The footpath skirts around the working compound, net fencing keeping the walker clear of the action. Cross the access road-way carefully, as there may be a lorry moving through. The path now wanders close to the beck (which can swell after heavy rain), continue by retained banks and some fallen trees the path moves on serenely as woodland way. Coming abreast Quarrybeck Cottage the path drifts right, up from the beck, to emerge at a kissing-gate onto the Brampton road.

5 Enter the facing road, signed 'Easby 1' and 'footpath to Brampton via The Ridge'. Follow the road over the brow and

Castlesteads from Brampton Ridge

downhill to find the bridle-lane signed left. The confined way leads by a simple seat, which revels in a lovely view from Craggle Hill and Haytongate round by the distant hills of Christianbury Crags and the Liddlesdale hills, to the table-topped Burnswark and Criffel to the west. Continue to a hand-gate into a sloping pasture, advance to where a footpath goes left at a kissing-gate. Ascend the young coniferous planting to the fence at the top, waymarking guiding on by the fence-end onto the main ridge-top path. Coppice woodland predominates, particularly after a pathway enters from the left. Go through the facing wooden squeeze stiles, a lane joins giving farm access to the pasture right.

Advance beside the mature row of beech trees. All along this section attention will be drawn northwards, across the green vale of the Irthing towards Walton and Castlesteads. Castlesteads, a large house situated upon the site of Camboglanna Roman Wall fort, has connections with the first 'Arthur' of Arthurian legend fame: Lucius Artorus Castus, a cavalry commander was garrisoned here in the second century AD. Passing a Woodland Trust sign the path exits the wood, via a metal kissing-gate, to proceed through the meadow with the hedge close left. The nearby beech trees have had mixed fortunes! A further kissing-gate brings entry into a very sandy lane leading down to a cottage.

6 The lane bends left but the walk goes straight ahead into the wooded hilltop park. Of the three obvious paths, take the right-hand way, this winds irresistibly to the summit of the hill. Surmounting the table-top is a very regal statue of the 7th Earl of Carlisle of Naworth Castle, who died in 1864. While every Tom, Dick and Harry admires the stone pavilion to the memory of the 9th Earl, set in the triangular green beneath the hill, only those with the puff to climb the little hill get a chance to admire this fine bronze sculpture. Trees inhibit the view, which is a pity in one sense,

7th Earl of Carlisle on The Moat

as there can be no doubt the site commands an advantageous prospect over the town of Brampton and surrounding countryside. The hill is known as The Moat, derived from motte and bailey, evidence of this dry ditch feature girdles the western and northern flank; an early medieval wooden defended house will have stood where the handsome Earl now resides.

In descent, uncoil your ascent to the point where, almost behind the statue, the first path veers away right. The path leads round by the ditch itself, to reach a fence. Turn left, descending the stepped path to meet a wall, turn left again, keeping the wall close right. The path next bears left to contour under the hill once more, take the next path right, leading back to the wall. While one may go through the inviting gap, down the steps, as a direct route to the town centre, the chosen way veers left again running down towards the road duly arriving beside the brown heritage sign. Again it is convenient to walk right

The Moot Hall in Brampton Market Place

into the town centre, passing the Brampton Playhouse and Co-op. Follow High Cross Street left into the Market Place, focused upon the handsome Moot Hall, containing the parish room and tourist information centre (TIC). Should you not wish to sample the delights of Brampton, carefully cross over the road onto the footway beside the Sands terrace and the Wilson Almshouses. At the Tree Road junction, cross over by the Sands Garage (formerly accessing the Staiths railyard), follow the footway up Station Road.

7 Immediately beyond the stone bridge abutments, the remnants of the old Dandy Line, and before Railhead Garage, cross to the kissing-gate and steps signed 'Station 1'. Proceed along the level cinder path, heading along the top of an embankment where once

The Dandy Line

plied a horse-drawn dandy wagon, carrying passengers to the main rail junction on the Carlisle/Newcastle Railway. Luxuriant growth can brush against the walker but frequent use tends to keep it at bay: thanks to cyclists, those exercising dogs, those accessing Rowbank Wood, and a few passengers using it as a nifty way to the train. The A69 by-passes Brampton and could have been the death knell to the track, but it has been accommodated in a concrete tunnel, permanently lit to prevent ambush. A long green cutting leads beside Rowbank Wood, paths delve right, into its quiet inner depths. The Dandy Line leads on, by a pond, to the two-sided platform, originally, passengers were able to alight directly onto the main line platform, though wooden fencing precludes such easy access now. The trail ventures to the station access gate. Cross the railway line via the handsomely painted footbridge.

BRAMPTON JUNCTION to HAYTONGATE |>>

8 Cross the railway line via the handsomely painted footbridge. Turn left, now upon The Dandy Line, via a kissing-gate and information panel, defining the pattern of paths in Rowbank Wood. Within a mile of blinkered walking the path is ushered off the embankment, down steps to a kissing-gate and onto Station Road in Brampton. **7** Follow the footway left, beyond the Tree Road junction

Talkin Tarn

coming alongside Wilson almshouses and the Sands terrace.
6 Cross the main road to the path sign directing 'To the Moat and Monument'. Follow the path leading left, above the road to meet a wall, then bear right and first left to regain the wall. Follow the wall up to meet a rising path, go right, ascend to the girdling path beside the moat. Turn right, curling round to finally complete the ascent, on the broad drive, to the monument on the plateau top. In descent, follow the drive down to the cottage at the head of a bridle-lane, **5** keeping forward to a kissing-gate.

Now in pasture, keep the ridge fence right to a metal kissing-gate right, entering the Woodland Trust Ridge Wood. Follow an undulating line of beech trees to cross a field access lane via facing squeeze stiles. Continue within the coppice woodland to a fence corner, hold this close right until guided by waymarking down leftwards through the young plantation to a kissing-gate. Go through, turn right to a bridle-gate entering a confined lane, which leads on down to the Easby road.

4 Turn right signed 'Quarry Beck', following the road to the junction and cross straight over to the metal kissing-gate, entering woodland. The path weaves on down by Quarry Beck, with fallen trees and water erosion challenging the retaining boards, as the path reaches the fenced compound of a stone cutting business. The path keeps close round by the fence and soon exits the woodland. It then briefly runs along the base of a steep pasture bank before re-entering the woodland at another kissing-gate. The path passes above an attractive waterfall before crossing a wooden footbridge rising over the dry mill leat to meet the Naworth road.

Turn left downhill, cross the road and walk over the old Abbey Bridge, as the modern road bridge is prosaic. **3** Bear right through the picnic site to the wicket-gate crossing the road to the facing hand-gate. Follow the River Irthing upstream to a tall finger-post, turn left across the meadow towards Lanercost Priory. Cross the stile and proceed beside the priory enclosure to a kissing-gate into the churchyard. Follow the gravel path round to a kissing-gate bearing right beside the wall to a wicket-gate. Cross the road, follow the footway left to the four-way junction. **2** Follow the lane right between the cottages as it bends left, and bear right up the drive to Haytongate **1** to link up with the National Trail – perhaps gaining refreshment at the specially resourced cabin through the hedge.

BRAMPTON JUNCTION to HYNAM WOOD (2)
6.2 km | **3.9** miles > **1.8** hours

8 Pass through the wicket-gate onto the road, turn right. Follow this for a third of a mile, beyond the pylon lines, to a footpath through a gate to the left signposted to 'Talkin Tarn'. A green track slips through a rushy dip at the head of a large marshy basin, formerly a mere, keep to the right-hand hedge to a kissing-gate into the woodland shielding Talkin Tarn.

9 Head straight on through the trees to the path on the shore. The formal path makes a gentle circumnavigation of the entire tarn, so you can go either way, but perhaps the café in the former boat club building will cause a preference to the right. The tarn would not be out of place at the heart of Lakeland. At any season, in any light, the visual delight of this mere will cause the visitor to pause and reflect on a sublime beauty. The café does a roaring trade during the summer season, the balcony view a special pleasure. Talkin Tarn and grounds were gifted by the Earl of Carlisle to the people of

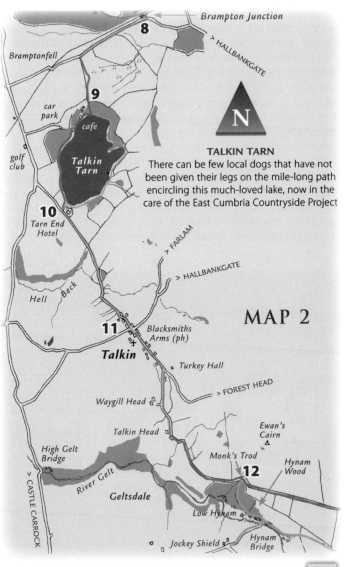

8

> Brampton Junction

Bramptonfell

> HALLBANKGATE

car
park

9

café

golf
club

Talkin
Tarn

N

TALKIN TARN
There can be few local dogs that have not
been given their legs on the mile-long path
encircling this much-loved lake, now in the
care of the East Cumbria Countryside Project

10

Tarn End
Hotel

> FARLAM

> HALLBANKGATE

Hell Beck

MAP 2

11

Blacksmiths
Arms (ph)

Talkin

Turkey Hall

> FOREST HEAD

Waygill Head

Talkin Head

Ewan's
Cairn

High Gelt
Bridge

Monk's Trod

Hynam
Wood

12

River Gelt

Low Hynam

Geltsdale

CASTLE CARROCK

Jockey Shield

Hynam
Bridge

Brampton over a century ago; at a little over a mile long, the walk around the shore is hugely popular with locals as well as visitors. Recent changes have brought the ownership and management of this Country Park into the hands of Carlisle City Council, and thus under the wing of the East Cumbria Countryside Project.

In many ways it has a rich social and natural history: the tarn is the home of one of the oldest rowing clubs in England, and casual boat hire is available for visitors to experience the truly lovely setting from its midst – it's an either oar choice! If you are in need of refreshment and the café is closed, set your sights on Talkin village a mile further on, where there is one of the best rural pubs in the area.

Follow the path along the western shore passing the boathouse close to the car park access, continuing by a willow bower and hand-gates almost to Tarn End Hotel, bear off right to the kissing-gate onto the road. A word of warning: the Tarn is plagued by blooms of blue-green algae, and is unsafe for swimmers.

The Blacksmiths Arms

The green road above Hynam Wood

10 Follow this lovely rural byway up into the village of Talkin, a matter of three-quarters of a mile distant. Entry into this attractive little village is by a chicane of houses. Passing the recently closed Hare and Hounds pub, and facing the small green at the cross roads, is the very much alive and kicking pub, The Blacksmiths Arms. The village-name has nothing to do with the propensity of inhabitants to intense conversation, rather is of purely Celtic origin, in modern Welsh it means 'forehead', possibly alluding to the brow-top situation of the village.

11 From the green, pass the pub and the charming Normanes-que parish church built in 1842. Reaching a minor road fork, bear right signed 'Talkinhead'. Pass the old primary school,set beneath a sandy ridge, the rigg formed by meltwater beneath an glacial ice-cap. Beyond the entrance to Whygill Head the road dips to Talkinhead, with a row of eight holiday cottage units in a converted barn beside the track. The tarmac gives way to a rougher road, an unclassified county road to be precise. This lonnen dips and rises with lovely views into the wooded depths of the Gelt above Castle Carrock. The far heather-clad fellside culminates on Hespeck Raise, an ancient burial mound on the ridge of Castle Carrock Fell leading to the unseen scarp of Cardunneth Pike above Cumrew, two further distinctively Celtic place-names.

12 Soon Hynam Wood is passed, with a bridleway signed right, down a track known as the Monk's Trod, possibly linking the meadow below with a retreat connected with Lanercost Priory – a monastic journey very similar to that just completed on The Roman Ring. A medieval bastle (defensible farmhouse) exists in the next meadow downstream beneath Talkinhead. Low Hynam is a collier's cottage dating from 1838. Continuing, the lonnen rises above the largely birch woodland with the great amphitheatre of Geltsdale opening ahead; watch out for blackcock, the enclosures to the right a favoured lekking ground. Across the valley the whitewashed cottages of Jockey Shield and Hynam Shield catch the eye. Strictly the name Geltsdale belongs to upper valley, the prominent breast of fell, beneath Tarnmonath, being the King's Forest of Geltsdale.

HYNAM WOOD to BRAMPTON JUNCTION |>>

12 The rough tracked lane sustains its superb views even after passing the top of the Hynam Wood, with lovely views down in the lower valley towards Castle Carrock, and beyond to Carlisle, with Blencathra and Skiddaw holding attention to the south. The lonnen dips and rises by the holiday cottage row at Talkinhead, join the tarmac road. This road leads past the old primary school to meet the minor road from Forest head, turn left to enter Talkin **11**. Proceed to the crossroads in the middle of the village, beyond the Blacksmiths Arms, and continue passed the old Hare & Hounds following the country road leading down to Talkin Tarn. Immediately beyond the currently vacant Tarn End Hotel **10** go through the kissing-gate on the right, descend to join the tarn-orbiting path at a hand-gate. Turn left, and follow the path via a kissing-gate to pass the café and gift shop building. Advance to a 'Brampton Junction' signpost guiding left, through the fringe of trees to a kissing-gate into a pasture field. **9** Keep the hedge close left en route to the kissing-gate onto the road. Turn right following the road to Brampton Junction, cross over the station footbridge left **8** en route for the Dandy Line path, leading left from the platform into Rowbank Woods.

HYNAM WOOD to HALLBANKGATE (3)
7.8 km | **4.9** miles > **2.5** hours

The lonnen makes a steady ascent with the higher fell at the head of Geltsdale rapidly becoming the focus of attention. The native woodland down in the valley contrasts with the wild heather moor boldly rising seemingly in tiers, above this, the last great valley of the Pennine chain. A large part of Geltsdale is either owned, or managed by the RSPB, and although there are currently no facilities for visitors, the reserve is famous for its wading birds such as curlew, woodland birds, particularly the pied flycatchers, and moorland species, including black grouse and hen harrier.

MAP 3

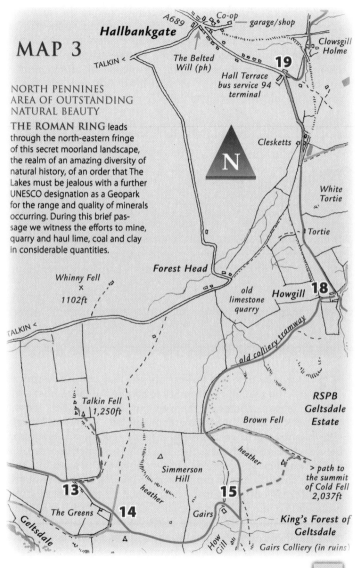

Hallbankgate

A689

Co-op

garage/shop

Clowsgill Holme

TALKIN <

The Belted Will (ph)

Hall Terrace bus service 94 terminal

19

NORTH PENNINES AREA OF OUTSTANDING NATURAL BEAUTY

THE ROMAN RING leads through the north-eastern fringe of this secret moorland landscape, the realm of an amazing diversity of natural history, of an order that The Lakes must be jealous with a further UNESCO designation as a Geopark for the range and quality of minerals occurring. During this brief passage we witness the efforts to mine, quarry and haul lime, coal and clay in considerable quantities.

N

Clesketts

White Tortie

Tortie

Whinny Fell × 1102ft

Forest Head

old limestone quarry

Howgill

18

TALKIN <

old colliery tramway

Talkin Fell 1,250ft

Brown Fell

heather

RSPB Geltsdale Estate

> path to the summit of Cold Fell 2,037ft

13

Simmerson Hill

heather

15

The Greens

14

Gairs

How Gill

Geltsdale

King's Forest of Geltsdale

Gairs Colliery (in ruins)

25

Passing through a gate, the track becomes open to the right with a nearby escarpment of old limestone quarrying visible to the right. To the left, sink hollows reveal the change from sandstone to carboniferous limestone under a blanket of peat. Doubtless attention will have been paid to the parade of cairns, nine in number, running along the skyline of Talkin Fell, up to the left. In passing through the next gate the green track forks.

HELVELLYN   SCAFELL PIKE   GREAT GABLE   BLENCATHRA   SKIDDAW

13 Given the time and inclination, you may consider a spur to visit the summit of Talkin Fell to admire the cairns from close quarters (above), and enjoy the view they command. Keep on the green track holding the wall close to your left. As this wall breaks left, follow it up to an intervening fence then, just a few paces before, climb carefully over the wall (this is normal practice but a stile would be appreciated). Follow the lip of the scarp to a stile in a wall giving access to the summit OS column and the brink-top cairns. The age of the cairns, is confirmed by the post-enclosure wall building remnants in the shallow quarry behind: local visitors piled up the stones, forming the distinctive currick cairns making a 'nine standards rigg' (the more illustrious name-sake stands above the Eden market town of Kirkby Stephen at the head of Swaledale).

Elsewhere in this area, standard curricks with genuinely antiquity exist, insofar as they are post-medieval shepherding landmarks: there is an opportunity to visit three of these, further up the valley beyond Gairs. One can understand why locals like to climb this little hill, with its breezy perspective down on the lower Eden plain to Carlisle, and the Solway Firth. Retrace your steps to continue.

The trail-focused walker will keep right, upon the close-cropped turf. Keeping the wall close right, pass a cottage ruin beneath an ageing ash. Soon after passing The Greens, an enchantingly remote little cottage lovingly maintained, powered and water-pumped by wind turbine: a scale of renewable energy that all would applaud. Though living in the valley below, the author knows one down-side, for when the wind really blows a gusty gale, under stress the turbine blades, emit the most awful, eerie, primeval moan.

14 At the enclosure wall-end, the green-way strides merrily forward, you'll spot that a regular path cuts right beside the wall, part of a locally popular scenic loop from Jockey Shield via Hynam Bridge. The green-way passes several old limestone quarried hollows, then links with a level track near the prominent cairn overlooking the meeting of Howgill Beck with the Gelt. From this point, the fell above is properly known as the King's Forest of

The bridleway approaching Gairs

Geltsdale. This was indeed a medieval hunting forest, though the more recent hunting has been with guns for grouse. However, even that is no longer practised, this area being part of the Geltsdale RSPB Reserve. Simmerson Fell, up to the left, is a gritstone scarp clothed in heather, a countenance that would not be out of place on the eastern edges of the Peak District.

Pass through a kissing-gate, the track draws closer to Howgill Beck curving to view the Gairs, a derelict dwelling formerly the homes of the local shepherd, and the gamekeeper. Up to the right notice the spoil banks and ruined structures connected with the Gairs Colliery. Turn acutely left. After some 150 metres the bridleway merges with the gently inclined Gairs Colliery tramway. Evidently the coal mined here was of an excellent quality, reputedly the mine only closed because the manager couldn't get to it with his car! The mine had been developed by the Earl of Carlisle and was operated with locomotives down the tramway via Howgill and Hallbankgate to Milton Junction. After being rebuilt several times, George Stephenson's famous 'Rocket' ended its working life here. The trackbed bends right and inclines slightly more steeply to meet the bridleway from New Water.

15 COLD FELL MOUNTAIN LINK
GAIRS TO HOWGILL   6.7 km | 4.2 miles > 2.8 hours

If you are considering adding the summit of Cold Fell into your expedition this is a significant moment – decision time! Cold Fell is worth every inch of the modest moorland climb, largely upon firm blanket bog. Being the northernmost two-thousand foot summit in the Pennine range, its position guarantees a superb view if you are fortunate to have good visibility.

While the colliery tramway progresses easily along the lower heathered slopes of Brown Fell to a gate – an alternative point to join the ascending ridge fence – the more attractive route breaks here GR 584557, currently marked lightly through the grass by a shepherd's quad bike track. Ascending, surprisingly dry-shod, to the first hint of heather, pass across the base of a jumble of boulders headed by a small cairn. Contour to the prominent cairn perched upon a small outcrop, a skyline landmark since you turned into the upper valley towards Gairs. This is a fine spot to view Geltsdale and

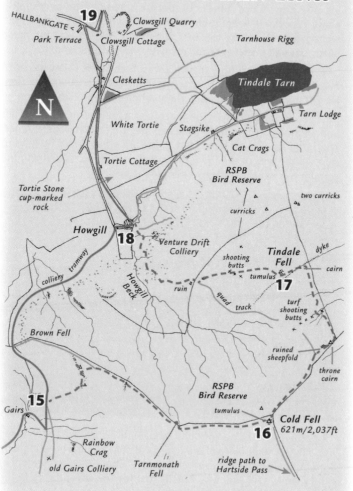

COLD FELL MOUNTAIN LINK

HALLBANKGATE ◄

19

Park Terrace

Clowsgill Quarry

Clowsgill Cottage

Tarnhouse Rigg

Clesketts

Tindale Tarn

Tarn Lodge

White Tortie

Stagsike

Cat Crags

Tortie Cottage

RSPB
Bird Reserve

two curricks

Tortie Stone
cup-marked
rock

curricks

Howgill

18

Venture Drift
Colliery

Tindale
Fell

dyke

cairn

shooting
butts

tumulus

17

colliery tramway

ruin

Howgill Beck

quad track

turf
shooting
butts

Brown Fell

ruined
sheepfold

throne
cairn

15

Gairs

RSPB
Bird Reserve

tumulus

Cold Fell
621m/2,037ft

16

Rainbow
Crag

old Gairs Colliery

Tarnmonath
Fell

ridge path to
Hartside Pass

the adjacent heather-clad hilltops of Simmerson; Talkin and the backing Castle Carrock Fells; the latter overtopped by Blencathra and Skiddaw. Walk a matter of 70 metres back, over tough grass, to join the ridge fence. Turn right, pursue a narrow trod over typical peaty moorland vegetation. A fence converges from the right, segregating the ridge-top of Tarnmonath Fell, an ancient name partly derived from the Welsh mynydd, meaning 'mountain'.

For more than a century the water resource of the valley has been harnessed by Carlisle City, drawing considerable quantities from New Water, though thankfully via boreholes rather than a dam.

It is easier to step over the fence you have been following, left and immediately right, to sidestep the taller convergent fence. The ridge fence next bends left, there are a few peaty hollows to skip. All the way to the the great tumulus of boulders marking the summit it is worth pausing to admire the views.

A gathering of some antiquity (above), the chaos has been given more than a semblance of order by local dentist, Jim Fotheringham, who built a substantial cairn and wind-shelter howff in memory of his dynamic son, Joe, who cruelly lost his life adventuring in the Caucasus Mountains of Russia. There is a real sense of continuity, the tumulus itself was established at some distant time, as a mark of ancestral remembrance. During the author's most recent visit, on an early September sunny Sunday, a small flock of fieldfares swooped by in migration. The view potential is tremendous: south towards Cross Fell keen eyes might spot the café at the top of Hartside Pass (sighted a smidgen to the right of the ridge fence), an infamous motorbike rendezvous – thankfully they can't make it here! Afternoon sun can glint on the burnished chrome of the serried ranks of machines.

Elsewhere the eyes may scan a wide horizon - binoculars a real bonus. To the south-west the Lakeland fells can be picked out, a crowded company. To the north-west, Criffel and the Southern Uplands lead the eyes right to Christianbury Crags, with White Preston and Gillalees Beacon, sites of a Roman Signal Stations to the north. Cold Fell marks the end of the Pennines, so correctly the Pennine Way should have ended here! But there are blessings that it doesn't, as the few folk who come, do so out of personal desire and a delight in solitary mountains. The author encountered one such connoisseur on that lovely day, Nick Leeming from Haltwhistle, an accomplished Northumbrian piper and all round outdoor man – such casual summit meetings are the meat and matter of a good day on the fell. [Furthermore, from that meeting Nick subsequently edited this guide, adding further dimensions to the prose]. The continuing ridge to Hartside is pure, peaty, Pennine moor, unsavoury and squelchy to the boot.

16 Leave the summit via the stile to the north, with fire beaters at hand - warning of the potential of peat fires and the need for their speedy suppression. The small cairn on the brow over to the left is an old shepherd's landmark, marking the eye line to the summit from Howgill, and is not a guide for walkers. Keep right, close to the gently descending fence, with quad bike tracks a sign of a visit from the staff managing the 12,000 acre Geltsdale RSPB Reserve. Notice the stripes on Midgeholme Fell, grouse moor heather kept young by cutting, not burning. Continue, passing a large sheepfold by a 'throne cairn', set tight beside the fence, the quad-track veers left. On reaching a fence junction, ignore the gate, and bear left. There is no path, keep the northward fence reasonably close to the right. 'Reasonably', as peaty groughs give cause to deflect left, especially where the line of old turf shooting butts is located. Eventually, a stone-embedded dyke slices across the ridge, follow it left to the small cairn, then to the substantial currick crowning Tindale Fell.

17 The currick is a fine edifice, set upon a tumulus that must be contemporary with the one on Cold Fell (see back cover). Travellers along the A69 can see it in the vicinity of Low Row, and mistakenly think they are looking at the summit of Cold Fell. The term currick is a variant of the Welsh 'carreg' meaning 'the rocks', hence the nearby village-name Castle Carrock. The instances of such place-names in this area is significant and points to a strong tradition of celtic individuality among the insurgent Anglian society; Croglin, Cumrew, Castle Carrock and Talkin are all from

Howgill from the Tindale Fell descent

these pre-Viking roots. OS maps proclaim this area of fell as Bruthwaite Forest, on a par with the King's Forest of Geltsdale, on the south-western slopes of Cold Fell. The RSPB has recently completed a large-scale woodland planting that runs around the steep hillside from Brown Fell to Stagsike — a new Bruthwaite Forest. If you do not visit the cairn, keep along the quad track on a north-westerly line into the combe. From the currick however, it is easier to follow the broad pathless ridge westwards, down to meet the quad track at a hurdle in the fence, close under a curious quartzite rib of rock. Lower down, the track has been cut as a shelf. Access the old colliery terrace of Howgill (see above) via a gate. A path destined for Stagsike and Tindale Tarn heads off right.

Gairs tramway

15 THE LOW ROUTE FROM GAIRS

Continue upon the colliery tramway, pass through a gate where the ridge fence intersects; an abundance of purple heather is a pleasing feature in late summer. Strictly, the bridleway follows the old wall line, tilting a little higher up the slope, but there is no gate in the fence where it crosses, so it has become redundant. Attention now switches to the old limestone workings about Forest Head. The track gently descends via a cutting, the tramway curves left over an embankment, but the path slips right. Go through a gate by a stone barn and pony paddock, pass the old colliery terrace of Howgill, via two gates.

18 Join the open track leading north from the hamlet, passing the curiously named cottage 'Tortie', descriptive of the adjacent pudding-shaped hill, like a tortoise. On meeting a tarmac road, note the Access Land information left. To the right a track leads to Tindale Tarn, an important site for migratory birds within the greater Geltsdale RSPB Reserve. Follow the road north by 'Clesketts', another old name alluding to woodland: watch the sudden brow in the road, cars can come unseen, locals always honk their horns! At Park Terrace ('Crossgates' on the bus timetable marking the easternmost terminal point on the regular Stagecoach service 94 from Carlisle), you may follow the road down into the village of Hallbankgate, to The Belted Will – an excellent pub, a Co-op Convenience Store, and a garage – soft drinks and confectionery.

19 Turn right over the cattle-grid following the open bridle track, access to the former Clowsgill limestone quarry, until parallel with Clowsgill Cottage (with a silent 'w') set back on the right. The footpath bears left. A track inclines, to pass beneath a gated bridge in the old mineral line embankment. Continue on the path via gates, passing in front of Clowsgill Holme Farm.

CLOWSGILL HOLME TO HYNAM WOOD |>>

Passing in front of Clowsgill Holme **20** go beneath the embankment via the gated bridge. Rising on a green track to meet a bridle-track facing a cottage, turn right to cross a cattle-grid at Park Terrace **19**. Turn left and follow the minor road, at a gate it becomes a rough surfaced track signed 'private road' to Howgill. **18** Enter the confines of the old colliery terrace via a gate, turn right and go through a paddock, via gates. On exiting turn left, onto the course of the old Gairs Colliery Tramway. Follow this, gently rising via cuttings to a gate marking the transition into the Geltsdale catchment. Keep along the bridleway, the tramway forks up to the old Gairs mine site **15**. As you come above the Gairs, cut back down sharp right joining a more regularly used path swinging left in passing the cottage, becoming a lovely green way. Passing through a kissing-gate continue to a fork, close to a lonesome cairn. Keep right, coming alongside a walled enclosure **14** pass the The Greens, solitary cottage, advance to a gate **13** into a lonnen.

This lane makes a steady descent en route to Hynam Wood **12** and Talkinhead. The rough tracked lane sustains superb views, towards Castle Carrock in the lower valley, and beyond to Carlisle, with Blencathra and Skiddaw to the south. The lonnen dips and rises by the holiday cottage row at Talkinhead, join the tarmac road. This road leads past the old primary school to the minor road from Forest Head, turning left enter Talkin **11**.

At the crossroads, in the middle of the village, The Blacksmiths Arms is a real treat. Proceed past the Hare & Hounds (no longer functioning), along the country road leading down to Talkin Tarn. Immediately beyond the Tarn End Hotel (currently vacant), **10** go through the kissing-gate on the right, descend to join the tarn-orbiting path at a hand-gate. Turn left, following the path via a kissing-gate to pass the café and gift shop building. Advance to a signpost 'Brampton Junction', guiding left through the fringe of trees to a kissing-gate into a pasture field. **9** Keep the hedge close left, head for the kissing-gate onto the road. Turn right, follow the road to Brampton Junction, crossing over the station footbridge left **8** en route for the Dandy Line path, leading left from the platform into Rowbank Woods.

HALLBANKGATE TO STOOP RIGG (4)
4.3 km | **2.7** miles > **1.3** hours

20 Following the access track from Clowsgill Holme, go through the old mineral line embankment (bridge removed). Within 70 metres bear off the track right, into the pasture. Keeping the ditch to the right, aim for the foot of the birch and rowan clothed bank. With the fence to the left, go along the continuing shallow bank to join the open track leading up to a cattle-grid and the main road. Turn right with the A689 to pass Coalfell Cottages. The end cottage is the office, and hub of the local RSPB Geltsdale Reserve that ranges up over Cold Fell. Plans are currently advancing to relocate the office to Stagsike, the old shooting lodge close to Tindale Tarn.

21 A public byway forks left at the Roachburn Colliery Memorial Seat – the first electric-powered pit in England - the seat records the bravery of two overmen who lost their lives in a vain attempt to save a drowning comrade in 1908. Follow the lonnen, originally the main road to Alston and the South Tyne, via a gate. After Fauld Farm barns it becomes a walled drove lane, beyond a further gate it is an open track leading to a gate and the barns of Greenside Farm. Briefly hemmed in by conifers, the track goes through a gate passing Greenside Nook, enters pasture via a gate, continuing as a damp byway, then becoming a sunken green-way beside a double fence.

22 At a four-way sign beside the foundations of a building, follow the bridleway part-left 'Stanniston', keep the fence close right along Folly Rigg. This district can be quite noisy, not so much from bleating of sheep, rather the roar of military training jets overhead. Pass through a gateway into a fenced passage with a conifer plantation to the left on Stoop Rigg.

Roachburn memorial at the parting of the old and new Alston road

STOOP RIGG TO CLOWSGILL HOLME | >>

23 A quad bike track helps confirm the direct westward route to a gate in a wall, rising gently over a ridge enter a fenced passage left of a conifer plantation on Stoop Rigg.

Emerge keeping the fence left to reach a four-way sign **22** (NB the westward direction is a fifth direction, not signed by a board, but by a 'button' nailed to the post itself), keep heading west towards the gate in the wall. Continue, with what is now a sunken green-way, to a gate and pass Greenside Nook. Hereon a firm track, via gates passes Greenside Farm reaching the A689 at the Roachburn Pit Memorial. **21** Follow the main road passing Coalfell Terrace, take a footpath, signed left over a cattle-grid.

Follow the track (destination Howard View), only into the hollow. Leave to the right, keeping the bank and fence of the birch-clothed slope close right. Continue alongside the open ditch. Joining an open track, **20** turn left, slip through the old mineral line embankment (bridge removed), pass on in front of Clowsgill Holme Farm, via gates.

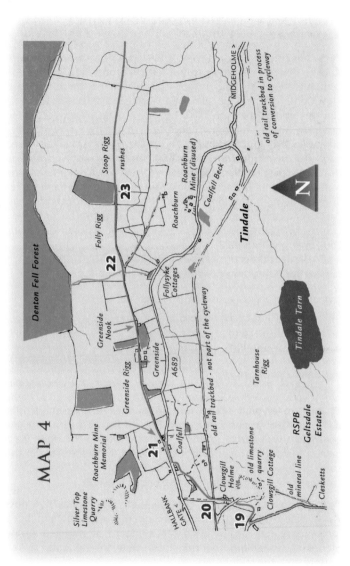

MAP 4

Silver Top Limestone Quarry

Roachburn Mine Memorial

Denton Fell Forest

Greenside Nook

Greenside Rigg

Greenside

A689

Folly Rigg

Stoop Rigg

rushes

Roachburn

Roachburn Mine (disused)

Coalfell Beck

MIDGEHOLME

old rail trackbed in process of conversion to cycleway

N

Follysyke Cottages

Tindale

Coalfell

Clowsgill Holme

old limestone quarry

Clowsgill Cottage

Tarnhouse Rigg

old rail trackbed - not part of the cycleway

HALLBANK GATE

RSPB Geltsdale Estate

old mineral line

Clesketts

Tindale Tarn

22

23

21

20

19

23 Pass through a gateway, entering a fenced passage with a conifer plantation to the left on Stoop Rigg. At the end continue ahead, keeping a right-hand bias along the rushy Stoop Rigg. Gently descending, go through a gate in a cross wall, maintain course through the rush filled-hollow, a quad bike track aiding progress. Aim for the broad fenced passage between two conifer plantations. Emerging, continue on a narrow trod, to a galvanised gate in a cross fence; with Winshields Crag on the Whin Sill visible in the far distance half-left. Advance to a gate, a fence right, puts the wall to the right. The access track from Haining House Farm comes in from the right; the term 'haining' meant land enclosed for hay. Pass over a cattle grid on Stanniston Hill and follow the farm track: two sheep creeps appear in the adjacent wall. Proceed via a gate.

Look over, and into the near valley, to the north; peruse the facing rigg, where a cup-marked slab of mystical Bronze Age significance is located (right) – no access unfortunately. Two further gates lead out onto a public road at a bend.

Regular cup-mark pitted sandstone slab

24 Turn left on the bend. Go through the first gate on the right bridleway sign 'Burnfoot'. The bridleway heads straight ahead to a wall corner, continue with the wall to the right, via a gate; a footpath crosses diagonally (hence the ladder-stile in the corner). However, proceed via two further gates, the Pennine Way crosses at the second gate (see also pages 120-122).

25 Keeping to the right of a low bank, pass a waymark post before slipping through an open wood. Descend by a further waymark post, noting the evidence of rigg-and-furrow ploughing straddling the ridge. Go through the gate at the bottom onto the minor road.

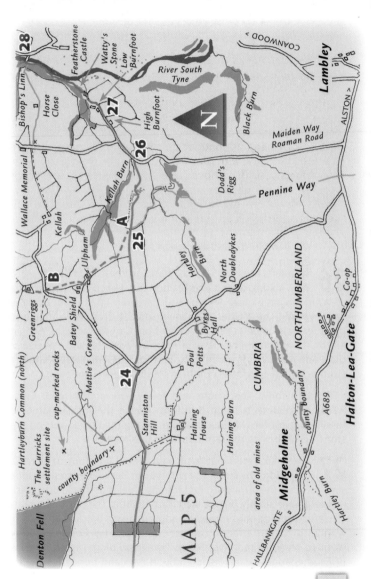

MAP 5

Fossil ferns at High Burnfoot

26 Turn left, the road approximates to the line of The Maiden Way, a Roman road. The Maiden Way linked the Roman forts of Whitley Castle, near Alston, and Carvoran (Magna) beside the Roman Wall. [The Maiden Way traversed the Cross Fell range into the Eden vale; joined the road south from Carlisle (now the A66) at Kirkby Thore Roman fort (Bravoniacum); made a second traverse of the Pennines over Stainmore, bound for, the legionary's administrative capital controlling Hadrian's Wall at York (Eboricum).]

The road forks, keep right and follow the access road. Cross Hartleyburn Beck to High Burnfoot. Notice the locally-gathered fossilised giant fern stalks, displayed among the flower pots on the stone bench beside the farmhouse door (above).

27 The road peters out as it passes Low Burnfoot. Traverse a footbridge re-crossing Hartleyburn Beck. The stream-name suggests that the term 'burn' is culturally older than 'beck', otherwise it would have simply been called Hartley Burn. The path now hugs the left-hand side of a tangled meadow of dense bracken and scrub; wonderful for butterflies on a warm summer's day. Continue to the wooded banks of the River South Tyne, providing a splendid view of Featherstone Castle. Set grandly in parkland beneath wooded banks, witness a mix of to the genuinely medieval defended tower with the romantic flamboyance of Victorian fantasy. Built around a courtyard, it was centred upon a thirteenth-century hall-house to which a pele tower was added in 1330. A period film-set, rooted in the turbulent past, a spooky charm pervades the whole environs, might there be ghosts... well wait for Pinkings Cleugh!

28 At times of excessively high water, this area must become difficult, the only recourse is to follow the road up Craigs Hill to the Hope Wallace Cross, erected on the spot where lovers parted before leaving for the Great War. Traverse the field passing the isolated cottage, Horse Close. Descend the stepped bank via a hand-gate to the Featherstone footbridge, a longer but no less scenic approach. The riverside path passes a weir, known for its leaping salmon, then weaves through to the Featherstone footbridge. Cross the bridge to a stile with a road beyond.

Featherstone Castle

28 Crossing the end of Featherstone footbridge, step down to the left, weave through the wooded banks close to the South Tyne. Emerge into a meadow generously decked with bracken, the path is reasonably well used, there should be no difficulty in making the footbridge over Hartleyburn Beck and the track passing Low Burnfoot **27**. This track becomes a public road passing High Burnfoot, re-crosses Hartleyburn Beck advancing to a road junction. Turn left, soon after crossing Kellah Burn find the bridleway sign at a gate on the right. **26** Go through, ascend the rigg, passing waymark posts either side of open woodland. Continue beside a low bank to a gate, the Pennine Way diagonally crossing the bridleway's westward march **25** | **A**. Keep the wall left, via two gates, then as the wall breaks left continue to a gate onto the road. **24** Turn left only a few metres, on the bend branch right through the gate adorned with the Haining House notice, and signed 'Greenside Road'. Follow the access track via a gate and then cattle-grid. Keep forwards with a wall right, to a gate. Now with a fence left, advance to a gate and an open pasture traverse to the fenced gap between matching plantations. Rushes more than hint to the damp nature of the pasture, but there is little real bog. A quad bike track helps confirm the direct westward route to a gate in a wall.

FEATHERSTONE FOOTBRIDGE TO HALTWHISTLE (6)
6 km | **3.7** miles > **1.8** hours

28 There are two basic options from this point. Either cross the footbridge and the road via stiles; rising through the parkland join the ascending Hall Bank road above Featherstone Castle, to the old Featherstone Park Station, on the former Alston line. At this point, with a car park right and the Wallace Arms only a matter of 150 metres further up the road, the South Tyne Trail cycleway may be joined, going left directly to Haltwhistle. Be warned, this involves walking entirely upon hard surfaces and the views from the trail are somewhat restricted.

Or opt for the primary route, keep to the wooded bank downstream to Featherstone Bridge, this is an utter delight but narrow in parts. Some landslipping, on the steep wooded bank, makes balance an issue. In due course this will be improved, but until then walkers

Featherstone Bridge

burdened with a heavy pack, or less surefooted, would be as well to cross the footbridge, follow the road left to Featherstone Bridge.

However, for those prepared to stick resolutely to the footpath, follow the path on round to cross the footbridge over Bishops Linn at the foot of Glen Cune. Reputedly associated with Bishop Nicholas Ridley of Willimoteswick, who became Archbishop of Canterbury. Glen Cune shows the Scottish variant of the Welsh 'glyn' meaning narrow valley, 'cune' is probably tautology from 'comb'.

Crow Wood begins as a stand of maturing pine, then as the path rises, becomes a mixed woodland. Steepening ground gives cause for cautious steps before emerging onto the road heading for the bridge. Built in 1775, Featherstone Bridge gracefully resolves the issue of the awkward disparity of fifty feet between the facing river banks.

29 Go through the gate onto the farm approach track, green sign Wydon Eals, footpath sign Wydon. Passing sheep pens the track comes alongside Pinkings Cleugh Burn and Deadmanshaw.

An horrendous tale is linked to this wooded dell, recounted in a famous ballad. Step back into the 17th-century when the Featherstonehaugh (pronounced 'Fanshaw') family resided at Featherstone Castle. They were catholic, so inter-marriage with protestants was not to be countenanced. Thus, when their daughter Abigail was courted by Richard Ridley of Hard Riding, her father insisted on a marriage with a catholic near neighbour, Blenkinsopp. The marriage contract required a church service at Haltwhistle, followed by a ride around the bridal estate, before a banquet in the castle. However, Hard Riding Dick and his men, knowing the ritual route, ambushed the party in Pinkings Cleugh; all the bridal entourage, including the bride herself were killed, spooky ghosts may linger from this jealous rage.

Proceed via gates, keeping on to the left of the farm buildings at Wydon Eals. Eals is a local form of 'isles', indicating that the river once was spread over a greater span than today, braided into various fluvial strands, with isles between; Wydon meant 'willow dene'. Beef cattle keep the environs of the farm buildings well and truly churned - muddy! From a stile left, rise by a wall, this becomes a fence before declining as a wall to a gate. Ford a tiny stream then

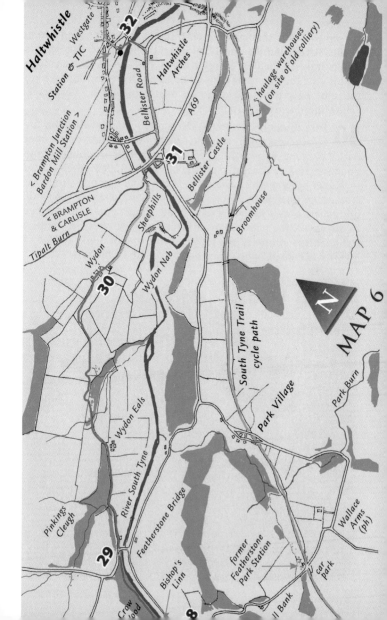

Haltwhistle

Station & TIC

Westgate

32

< Brampton Junction
Bardon Mill Station >

Bellister Road

Haltwhistle
Arches

A69

haulage warehouses
(on site of old colliery)

31

Bellister Castle

< BRAMPTON
& CARLISLE

Broomhouse

Tipalt Burn

Sheephills

Wydon

Wydon Nab

30

N

MAP 6

South Tyne Trail
cycle path

Wydon Eals

Park Village

Park Burn

River South Tyne

Featherstone Bridge

Pinkings
Cleugh

former
Featherstone
Park Station

car
park

Wallace
Arms
(ph)

29

Bishop's
Linn

Crow
Wood

8

ascend the bank shelf angling up through the open woodland to a stile. Skirt round the small hollow and follow the fence right to a stile. Traverse the field straight ahead, early on passing a trough set into the top of a re-entrant, to go through a gate with a wall to the right. Keep the fence left to the next gate joining a farm track. Follow this down to Wydon Farm.

30 Pass through (or stay B&B?), continue via gates, along the farm access road, cross the cattle grid. After the power lines notice the long slope right, known as Sheephills – popular after a good snowfall for tobogganing: the dip slope of Wydon Nab, a hard rock spur around which the River South Tyne contorts. The drive crosses the Tipalt Burn coming close to the A69, en route to a cattle grid giving access to the Bellister Road, almost opposite the drive to the castle. The name Bellister means 'the fine site'. The castle, a National Trust property, has its ghost too, that of the 'Grey Man of Bellister', a minstrel who was mauled to death by hounds.

The signal box at Haltwhistle Station

Centre of Britain Hotel

31 Instead of crossing the grid switch immediately right, along the concrete passage leading under the road bridge. *At times of high water this can be submerged. When necessary take the earlier path, off the farm lane signposted at a stile prior to coming alongside the A69, this leads under the west side of the bridge at a slightly higher level. From there follow the path up steps and along a lane to either, wander into town beside main street, or switch back right, by the barrier, over the bridge to regain the primary route on Bellister Road.* The primary route on the east side, curves up to become a tarmaced lane. Pass through a hand-gate onto the truncated Bellister Road, follow this to the second bridge, a grand old green and cream painted pedestrian span: your 'Welcome to Haltwhistle' confirmed underfoot.

32 Bear up left to inspect the handsome signal box, a galleon in dry dock. Cross the rail bridge, turn left passing the town's Tourist Information Centre, housed in the station's old ticket office - a busy hub for Hadrian's Wall information. Leave the station, pass the bus stop in Station Road, signed 'Town Centre'. Cross the former main road at the Railway Hotel, enter Westgate, the principal shopping street leading via Main Street into the Market Square.

The **Haltwhistle Walking Festivals** are held twice a year, usually in May and October when a keen band of local volunteers 'The Friends of the Rings' share with visitors their intimate knowledge of the area. The walks are carefully chosen to give a mixture of length and rigour. Many of these walks are themed – A Full Moon Experience, Finding the Source of the Tyne, (three walks over three days), An exploration of 400 years of coal mining remains, Youth walks, Walks for the visually impaired, are just a few examples. Shorter evening walks, evening talks and events are also arranged for those staying in the area overnight. The reference to the 'Rings' relates to the collection of well-documented local walks, 'The Haltwhistle Rings' that form the basis of the 'friends' weekly walks. For information on these walks, the Walking Festivals, and the regular Wednesday walks to which all are welcome, please contact the **Haltwhistle Partnership** on 01434 321 242.

HALTWHISTLE TO FEATHERSTONE FOOTBRIDGE | >>

Pass along Westgate, bear left, down Station Road stride onto the station platform. **32** Cross the pedestrian bridge over the railway following the footway left, by the signal box. Turn right, crossing the broad pedestrian bridge spanning the River South Tyne, at the road junction turn right. Follow Bellister Road beside the flat meadows of Bellister Haughs, the road is almost devoid of traffic, truncated by the A69 bypass. Directly after a second pedestrianised bridge right, go through the intervening gate, the road soon becomes a concrete lane curving under the trunk road bridge: note the gabions, minimising the effect of the river's exuberance during occasional flooding. The lane emerges at a hand-gate prior to a cattle grid, **31** turn left. Follow the farm road to Wydon Farm **30** pass through the farmyard via gates onto the track. Rising, go through the facing gate off the line of the track. Keep the fence right to another gate. Traverse the open pasture, skirt to the right of a re-entrant hollow, by a trough, to a stile in the corner. Keep the bank fence left, skirt round a small re-entrant to a stile.

Angle half-right, down the open wood to a small bank, follow this down to a ford and subsequent gate. Keep the wall, then gate left. Descending to Wydon Eals Farm pass on through the muddy environs via gates, onto the access track, which leads to a gate beside Featherstone Bridge. **29** Walk up the road 25 metres, a footpath sign guides left into Crow Wood. After 120 metres watch for an area of slumped ground, giving comfortable going for a few strides on the steep wooded bank. The path shortly descends weaving through the pines to reach a footbridge over Bishops Linn, continue to reach the end of Featherstone footbridge **28**.

HALTWHISTLE TO HALLPEAT MOSS
4.3 km | **2.7** miles > **1.3** hours

(7)

Haltwhistle is a lively, convivial little town, which retains something of its colliery community identity; listen to the speech you'll hear a very west Tynedale version of Geordie - people say 'haveent' whereas in Newcastle they would say 'hivvint', 'cood' instead of 'cud' and 'eet' instead of 'it'. Situated between the confluence of the Tipalt and Haltwhistle Burn with the South Tyne, the place-name means 'high ground by a watersmeet' from haut twyzell. Though our American cousins can be excused for their jovial quip when alighting from the train... "Is this Whistlestop?" Until the coming of the railway the town was often pronounced Hoddissel. Before the 19th-century the compact town had lain east of the church, far removed from the Tipalt.

Visitors are very much welcomed, there are plenty of shops to entice and restock, and in addition to the train, regular east/west bus services ensures easy access to the outside world. As you reach the small Market Square your eyes might alight upon the information boards and signs that pronounce this to be The Centre of Britain. The Black Bull Inn close by is the best haven for real ale in town, with good food and a warm fire. Further along Main Street is the Centre of Britain Hotel (formerly the Red Lion Inn), the smartest haven, and the Manor Hotel (B&B), formerly the actual manor house.

Note the wall plaques in the vicinity, proudly proclaiming that the buildings they adorn are, at their core, either bastles or peles.

Bastles: defended farmhouses, with accommodation on the first floor accessed via a wooden ladder, drawn up at times of threat, the animals lived in the windowless byre underneath protected by a stout door. Bastles kept the family safe from all but the most determined raiders, and keeping the animals below had the added advantage their body heat rising to warm the house as well – fragrant 'green' (or is that brown?) centre-heating.

Peles: tower houses, again for protection against the marauding reivers. The remnants of a pele can be clearly seen at the Centre of Britain Hotel. 13th-century raids by Scottish Reiving clans made life quite hellish, hence the need for such protection.

One should remember that under Pax Northumbria, instigated by the Anglo-Saxons, Northumbria extended as far as what is now Strathclyde (Edinburgh being named after the Northumbrian King Edwin): neither the Wall, nor the present Border were recognised as frontiers. The Normans ruined everything: Edward Longchamps and Robert the Bruce, who both had Norman French as their first language, created the present Border by way of their disputes. Reiving really came into its own in Elizabethan times, when Elizabeth's parsimony and Scotland's weakness in policing the Border allowed the more unruly families, especially the Elliots and Armstrongs of Liddesdale, and the Robsons of (North) Tynedale to get out of hand. As MacDonald Fraser noted in his book, 'Steel Bonnets', it also allowed the authorities on either side to have almost instant access to an aggressive militia, should an 'official' incursion take place from the other side. Over the course of centuries the Tudors neglect of the border led to petty feuding spilling into wider conflicts, and the polarity of Scottishness and Englishness became an excuse for family or clan-based aggression. So from the Roman frontier came Scottish borderland strife.

The Haltwhistle of today is calm enough, it grew in the 18th-century as an industrious coal mining centre, the area brimming with deposits. Indeed, up until ten years ago coal, laying a matter of metres under the surface, was being dug and sifted from Plenmeller Moor, while close to town, levels and shafts ventured to the various coal beds in the South Tyne Colliery. The Roman Ring cuts across Haltwhistle Burn but there is every good reason to venture all the way up this dell as far as the Military Road, and beyond to the Wall itself, to discover evidence of its mining past.

33 Follow the pavement from the Market Place passing the Centre of Britain Hotel to bear left, by Town Hall Crescent, rising on a cobbled footpath into Fair Hill. Keep right, and immediately after Fairfield Park turn left, 'private road' sign. 30 metres ahead a kissing-gate guides into a confined path leading down by a recreation ground into the wooded dell of Haltwhistle Burn, via steps. Cross the footbridge advancing to a four-way sign.

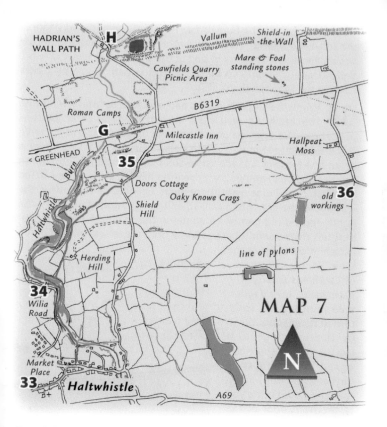

Turn left signed 'Willia Road'. Pass a securely fenced depot in an old quarry, and building remnants associated with the old South Tyne Colliery and later the South Tyne Fireclay Company. Fireclay was mined (shale associated with the coal measures), ground up, and made clay for pipes and bricks, using the salt glazing technique still used at the nearby Errington Reay Pottery in Bardon Mill.

Ignore Willia Road, keep to the east bank of Haltwhistle Burn. The path is the track bed of a narrow gauge railway that brought gravel from the Whin Sill at Cawfields, on the Wall, down to the rail head at Haltwhistle. The burn and the path make a sharp bend to the left.

Look for dipper on the burn. After the bend, the path forks; ignore the left-hand fork to a second footbridge, advancing straight on beside a wall, the remains of one of the three watermills that once derived energy from the burn. Find a footpath sign 'The Doors' right, at the foot of a flight of stone steps.

34 Climb the steps, in excess of one hundred, latterly following the brink-top wall right to a hand-gate. Enter pasture, now above the wooded gorge, look for buzzards, sparrow-hawks, fieldfares and redwings in winter. Follow the fence passing under a pylon line to reach a ladder-stile. You may be fortunate enough to see Herding Hill Farm's distinctive little black Dexters, a rare breed of British cattle, grazing in these fields. Bear half-left following the wall above the gorge to a wall-stile. Turn half-right glancing by the lightly fenced old quarry, continue up the shallow hollow to bear part-left over a semi-quarried brow on a green way providing an excellent prospect of the Whin Sill ridge either side of Cawfields Quarry. The path leads to a ladder-stile onto the road, turn left, passing down by Doors Cottage to a ladder-stile on the right, signed 'Hallpeatmoss'. A further 250 metres along the road would bring you to the front door of the Milecastle Inn, where the AD 122 bus stops, and, across the Military Road, an easy connection with the Roman Wall and car part at Cawfields.

35 A green track leads from the ladder-stile onto the rough grazing land

Old engine chimney in Haltwhistle Burn

north of Oaky Knowe Crags, initially slanting slightly leftward in rising, drawing closer to a wall. The path weaves through an area pock-marked with the old coal bellpits. The Whin Sill ridge dominates attention to the north from Mucklebank Crag, in the west to Winshields Crags, in the east with Great Chesters, Cawfields featuring nearby. As the wall is lost stick with the clear track, eventually diminishing to an indefinite trod on encountering an old enclosure bank. Keep beside this low bank for some 100 metres then bear half-right, soon picking up a clear, but narrow path leading via rushes to a ladder-stile beside a narrow gate in a wall. The path strictly ascends the bank ahead to join a green track beneath the old quarried scarp, though one can just go left picking up the green way as it veers through the grassed over spoil banking. Keep the wall of a camping field, associated with the Hadrian's Wall Caravan and Camping Site at Hallpeat Moss, to the left reach a gate onto the road.

HALLPEAT MOSS TO HALTWHISTLE |>>

With the Hadrian's Wall Caravan and Camping Site at hand, leave the road left, **36** go through a gate signed 'Haltwhistle'. Initially with the camping field wall right, the green track leads along the base of a scarp with rake excavations and green spoil bank. Watch for the sharp unwaymarked right turn, down the short bank to a ladder-stile beside a narrow gate in the wall. The path steps through a rush-filled ditch and advances to step over a low bank (old field boundary). Bear left, picking up a green path that becomes a more definite green way track. Weaving through an area of old coal bellpits with a wall close right, the path latterly declines to a ladder-stile onto the road 250 metres south of the Milecastle Inn.

35 Turn left, ignore the first ladder-stile on the right, rise past The Doors Cottage to the second ladder-stile and cross. Proceed on a green way, slipping over the shallow quarried brow. Be alert, keep right at the next nick. Descending the hollow keep the lightly-fenced old quarry to the right to reach a wall-stile. Continue beside the pasture wall above the wooded gorge, latterly drifting half-left to a ladder-stile. Keep the new fence close right, down under the pylon lines to a hand-gate. The path goes right descending a long flight of stone steps, in excess of one hundred!

34 At the foot turn left, following Haltwhistle Burn down past the old colliery/brickworks, through pines and birch now occupying the old railyard of the colliery, to the four-way sign. Turn right over the footbridge, ascend the short flight of steps then bear left into a confined path beside the recreation ground. Proceeding uphill emerge at a kissing-gate, via a short private road right onto Fair Hill, Haltwhistle. When the line of cottages on the left of the road gives way to a grass bank, turn left. Follow the cobbled path downhill by Town Hall Crescent right into the Main Street leading by the Centre of Britain Hotel and the Market Place. **33** Continue through the shopping street of Westgate en route to the railway station.

HALLPEAT MOSS TO CRANBERRY BROW (8)
1.6 km | **1** mile > **0.5** hours

36 Turn right up the gentle rise of the road progressing along a straight stretch. Ignore the first finger post left, continue to a public right-of-way' sign directing left. At a gate at the right-hand bend, embark on the ridge-top hardcore track with a wall to the left. Notice the vertical base stone construction intermittently replicating the cap running along the top of the wall. Unless you wish to make an early direct link to Once Brewed across the rough pasture, ignore the ladder-stile left at the next wooden gate. Continue to the next gate, enter a lane and subsequently a road from Cranberry Brow farm.

CRANBERRY BROW TO HALLPEAT MOSS |>>

37 From the lane end at Cranberry Brow pass through a gate, continue upon the open track along the shallow ridge-top, via two gates to emerge onto a minor road. Turn right and, following a short descent, with the Hadrian's Wall Caravan and Camping Site at hand, leave the road left, **36** through a gate signed 'Haltwhistle'.

CRANBERRY BROW TO HARESBY LONNEN (9)
7.7 km | **4.8** miles > **3** hours

37 Maintaining the ridge-way the road leads straight down from Cranberry Brow farm to a road junction and turns left. Note the 1935 Jubilee Seat, a stout wooden bench installed by the local Rural District Council that has urvived the elements and modest use extremely well, The Roman Ring will doubtless bring it a new

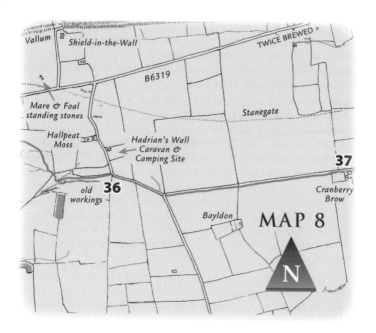

flush of aching limbs! The road leads ultimately to Once Brewed with its National Park Visitor Centre and Youth Hostel not forgetting the adjacent Twice Brewed Hotel. So while it can be considered a route to Steel Rigg; walkers are better served by footpaths from this spot, via Waterhead and Winshields Farm.

38 After 30 metres a 'public footpath' sign directs right along an access lane to Layside, ahead the heather-capped ridge of Barcombe commands skyline attention. A stile ushers the re-routed footpath out of the lane to the left some 100 metres short of the cottage environs. In view to the north: the roller-coaster line of the Whin Sill ridge with Sycamore Gap prominent. A path mown in the pasture guides walkers to a fence stile level with the end of the buildings. Angle half-right, wide of the tennis court and past a rail freight wagon, to a ladder-stile into the edge of a young deciduous plantation. Crossing a stile leave the woodland keeping a fence close right. At the next stile the path dips into a wooded dell with a muddy stream to cross at the bottom. Clamber up to a stile into a pasture. Pass across the slope, right of Kit's Shield's island cattle shed, to a stile at the head of a stream. Go through the open bushes, contour the next pasture to a stile in the thick hedge, obscured until you get quite close.

39 Entering a rough-tracked lane turn left, uphill. Beware of mountain bikers hurtling down this hill as you trudge up it! Levelling through a wooden gate, the track continues unenclosed across a pasture with a good view right down to Vindolanda, excitement mounts! At the next gate emerge onto The Stanegate Roman road, with a tarmac surface and in use as the main approach to this famous Roman site. The single-tracked road can be very busy at times, leaving the walker awkwardly exposed – keep alert. Some 200 metres to the left stands Causeway House, a Landmark Trust 'holiday let' property, with an authentic heather divot turf roof. Continue to the western car park entrance to the Vindolanda Trust's hugely popular estate.

The whole Vindolanda story is a source of fascination and is a jewel in The Roman Ring: for me it rates as a 'must visit', it certainly is a most enriching experience. The basic route follows the narrow lane continuing along the Stanegate into the valley, however, if you visit Vindolanda just re-join Stanegate in pursuance of your easterly journey.

Vindolanda and Barcombe from the west

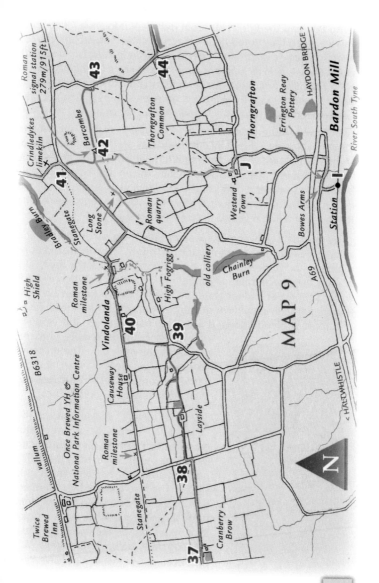

MAP 9

The BBC and the British Museum did the Vindolanda PR no small service when they voted their collection of 'writing tablets' the top historic treasure in Britain. The tablets are indeed fascinating, with more than 1,900 deciphered, they have revealed the daily affairs of Roman life just prior to the construction of Hadrian's Wall, a priceless insight into this long lost garrison society: the tablets can be accessed on line via http://vindolanda.csad.ox.ac.uk

Vindolanda Stanegate Roman fort and civilian settlement, Carvoran Roman Army Museum and the Stanegate/Wall fort of Magna at the western end of the Whin Sill, are owned and run by The Vindolanda Trust. It is Trust policy to run annual excavations during the summer months at their Vindolanda site: at present the only place in the World Heritage Site that you can regularly see the Roman past being revealed in front of your eyes.

The fort, vicus and a bathhouse have already been excavated, and other site details are constantly coming to light. Their reconstructions of timber and stone fort walls help to bring aspects of the site to life, stirring the imagination of young and old. The site is rich in fresh water springs, abundant water for the extensive Roman baths, a feature not seen at many of the higher Wall forts. The water created anaerobic soil conditions, preserving many leather and wooden items, giving the incredible finds on display in the museum. The museum also has an excellent teashop, and the gardens contain reconstructions of small Roman temples and shrines.

40 For those sticking with the lane, it does have one major monument all to itself, the Chesterholm Milestone (left). Secreted in the valley just beyond Codley Farm, it stands shyly in the field accessed via a ladder-stile to the left. Sheltered by trees and thorn bushes, it is undisturbed since its erection beside the Roman military thoroughfare, before the Roman Wall was even a twinkle in Hadrian's eye!

Follow the road uphill passing the eastern entrance to Vindolanda and its car park. Rise to the road junction, the steep heather clad slopes of Barcombe ahead rimmed by a quarried edge with clear evidence of Roman activity and graffiti (accessed from the ridge-top). Turn left, following the road in a north-easterly direction.

41 Coming close to the next junction locate a stile to the right. Before crossing, take a moment to both look over the wall to the left. A hollow-way runs away from a stone culvert, developed as a drain from a lead mine, enlarging the course of the Stanegate which here regains the modern road. Further north, beyond the junction, one might visit the impressive stabilised Crindledykes limekiln. The Stanegate might be thought a simple option en route to Newbrough. While a few history-enthused walkers may be tempted to follow this Roman engineered back road, via the old Morwood colliery, above Grindon Lough – a famous birding site, then via Settlingstones Witherite mine – the unique source of barium for diagnostic barium meals; your better bet is to go right onto Barcombe, as this is walkers' country *par excellencé*.

Cross the stile and follow the path signed 'Thorngrafton' easing up the slope. At the brow a shallow bank guides right, along the edge, the footpath heads on through the bracken breach to a gateway in the ridge wall. However, walkers should have two other objectives in mind. Firstly, the main route aims half-left onto the summit knoll, surmounted by an old Ordnance Survey pillar.

42 This is a Roman signal station. Look west, espy Stanegate's straight course, quite clearly aligned to this spot, so it was a Leyline too! Before continuing with the route consider a ten minute diversion onto the Barcombe spur, perhaps you'll have spotted the prominent standing stone on the horizon earlier. Take the time to stride south-west along the ridge to visit this monument, in a former life may have been the base of a cross, or even be the remains of a Bronze Age cup-marked rock. The Long Stone was erected in the 19th-century to the memory of nine colliery workers who lost their lives in the Chainley Burn mine. The mine, yielding award-winning quality coal, was situated on the southern slopes of Barcombe, spoil issuing from the adit in view from Vindolanda. Like the Roman Quarry, a little way down the ridge to the south, this is a superb

viewpoint over Vindolanda. To visit the Roman Quarry weave through the shallow quarries on the ridge-top to a part-broken hurdle in the ridge crossing wall, a clear path continues through the bracken and luxuriant heather, down the ridge (see opposite and front cover) to the next rise.

On the western flank of this rise is the quarry with undecipherable graffiti, a punch-marked phallic (above) perhaps the day's work of one soldier seeking to bring good luck to the fort, and a vertical line of three Lewis slots, cut in readiness for levering the rock from the face. You'll notice that an irregular chunk is missing below, perhaps the last rock removed by Roman hands.

Return to the signal station. Walkers choosing to link with The Roman Ring from the train may alight at Bardon Mill Station – stopping trains less than frequent – and venture onto Barcombe direct via West End Town and Thorngrafton Common (see map for directions). From the signal station, set amongst a bed of heather, head east slipping through bracken holding to the north side of the ridge. Pass evidence of shallow quarrying and what looks like a cup-marked rock, there is little more than the odd sheep trod as a clue to a path. Coming close to the roadside wall join a firm path leading down to the right and through a gateway. Go smartly left to a ladder-stile, thereby joining the minor road.

43 Turn right following the road, that enjoys lovely views of adjacent heather slopes and south over the South Tyne valley towards the Allen gorge. The road dips, then as it rises find a 'Public Byway' signposted left, this is Haresby Lonnen.

HARESBY LONNEN to CRANBERRY BROW |>>

Haresby Lonnen issues into a minor road, **44** turn right ascending north with heather moor most notably to the right. Arriving at a wall-stile on the left signed 'Thorngrafton' **43** cross and slip through the narrow gateway close right through the rushes. Ascend the sheep path parallel to the roadside wall onto the ridge, bear left with no hint of a path through the heather, later bracken, leading neatly to the Ordnance Survey pillar **42** on the Roman signal station at the top of Barcombe. Descending find the footpath trending north, down the bank to a wall-stile onto the road. **41** Turn left following the road to the junction, turn right descending into the Chainley Burn valley passing the eastern entrance to Vindolanda – don't lightly dismiss the opportunity of a visit, loop back onto the Stanegate road from the western entrance car park. The Stanegate re-joins the lane close to Chesterholm Milestone, continue past Codley Farm ascending as a narrow walled lane to the popular western entrance to the famous 'must visit' site.

Keep forward until a bridleway signs left **40** via a recessed gate. Traverse the open field on Kingcairn Hill to a wooden gate entering a lane, becoming a rough track as it descends. A matter of metres before a branch lane find a stile **39** tucked into the dense hedge to the right. Traverse the pasture to a stile lurking through the bushes, continue keeping to the left of Kit's Shield, the bank-top cattle shed/ yard, to a stile. The path dips into the dell crosses a muddy burn and clambers up to a stile. Keep the fence close left to a further stile, enter a young deciduous plantation. Emerging over a ladder-stile,

Vindolanda from the Roman quarry

angle half-right to a stile in a fence, level with the end of the adjacent buildings at Layside. A mown strip guides up to a stile left, into the access lane, follow the lane right to the minor road.

38 Turn left to the next junction by a seat. Turn right rising easily up the straight road to Cranberry Brow farm **37** and beyond to a gate where the lane opens to a ridge-way track.

Looking south to the Allen Banks gorge from the east end of the Barcombe ridge.

HARESBY LONNEN-END TO HALL BANK (10)
3.9 km | **2.4** miles > **1.2** hours

44 Striding out along Haresby Lonnen, a lovely country lane, you'll feel blissfully far from the madding crowd. Early on heather moor holds attention left with a shelter belt of trees right, then cattle pasture flanks the lane.

As a conifer strip is passed on the left, see north the great marshy expanse of Muckle Moss, an important valley-mire National Nature Reserve (the name literally means the 'big bog'). Then comes the recently felled conifer plantation 'Pit Covert', the wood-name a further hint to the underlying reserves of coal extensively shaft mined in this area, and for which there is surprisingly little residual trace.

45 Coming onto a roughly tarmaced roadway with five tonnes weight-limit – a caution for the well-being of Honeycrook

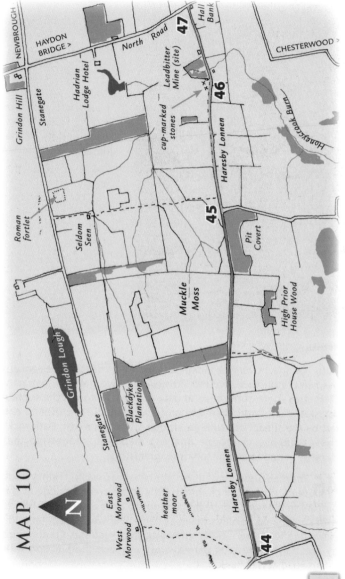

MAP 10

N

NEWBROUGH

HAYDON BRIDGE >

CHESTERWOOD >

North Road

Grindon Hill

Stanegate

Hadrian Lodge Hotel

Leadbitter Mine (site)

Hall Bank

47

46

cup-marked stones

Roman fortlet

Seldom Seen

Haresby Lonnen

45

Grindon Lough

Muckle Moss

Pit Covert

Honeycrook Burn

Stanegate

Blackdyke Plantation

High Prior House Wood

East Morwood

West Morwood

heather moor

Haresby Lonnen

44

Haresby Lonnen looking east

Burn bridge, over-burdened backpackers need not concern themselves on this account! Advance via two gates, a matter of 30 metres short of the second gate ponder the top of the solitary wayside stone, and then the more substantial rock over to the left by the sheepfold, with an eroded font in its midst. Both rocks show evidence of Bronze Age cup-markings, suggesting that Haresby Lonnen has a history from prehistory!

46 The road dips by woodland, site of a sheep wash in Honeycrook Burn, notice the charming little stone-arched bridge in the pasture to the right. To the left among the trees a derelict mine site with spoil banks, locally known as dams. This was Leadbitter Mine extracting lead and latterly, zinc until sixty year ago. Continue up by a cottage with a tall conservatory to reach the junction with North Road at Hall Bank.

Descending with the road by Cubstocks turn left by Hall Bank **47** signed 'Thorngrafton Common'. Follow this road down to cross Honeycrook Burn, rising to a gate. **46** The lightly tarmaced road leads on to a second gate then as the road bends left, **45** continue ahead within the 'No Through Road' this is the public byway Haresby Lonnen, which is followed through to the next road, a shade under two miles distant.

HALL BANK TO NEWBROUGH

5 km | **3.1** miles > **1.7** hours

(11)

47 To the left within half-a-mile find Hadrian Lodge Hotel, and a smidgen over two miles the Old Repeater Station bunkhouse accommodation for the Wall with café refreshments for passing walkers. Beyond, a link to the Wall Path at Sewingshields Farm, and the lonely track to Stell Green linking to the Moss Troopers' Trail. However, our trail now leads right up the road by Cubstocks.

48 At the cross-roads, notice that the sign right indicates the hamlet of Chesterwood, a name clearly referring to former ruined Roman buildings. However, our route goes left, marching on through the old colliery hamlet of New Alston, as the road bends sharply right, continue forward into Fell Lane.

49 Walkers disembarking from the train at Haydon Bridge will join the route here (see Haydon Link p.127). Fell Lane provides fine views south-east across the broad wooded South Tyne valley. Passing Fell House, not the traditional house abode one might expect on this spot – that was burnt – but an orderly stylish bungalow. Advance to a sharp left bend, the view east over the Newbrough vale towards Warden Hill is exceptionally pleasing. The rough tracked lane zig-zags down, then climbs by Fell Cottage with its proportionate wind turbine, charming garden and enviable view: formerly a shepherd's long-house. The rough surfaced lane begins to descend, but watch left for a footpath sign 'Stonecroft' at a gate, before a strip of conifers. Go through, follow the field edge down to a stile beside a large boulder. Step onto the road, with cottages left, this is Stanegate Roman road, watch for traffic speeding down the hill.

50 Bear right a few paces to cross a stile on the left, footpath sign 'Stonecroft'. Take a long diagonal line down the large pasture bank aiming for the stile in the far corner. Walk over the footbridge spanning Newbrough Burn at Bankfoot, with its hens and bees and lovely honey for sale! Follow the access track right to join the road, continuing right meet up with Stanegate once more. Bear left following road with the ghosts of marching Romans, down to St Peter's church.

51 Enter the churchyard via the step-stile beside the lych-gate signed 'Newbrough Hall'. The church is built on the foundations of a major, and as yet unexcavated Roman fort associated with Stanegate. The rounded north-west corner wall of the churchyard is built on the fort banking. Bear to the right of the church on a path leading to a wicket-gate. Enter a park-like pasture rippled by rigg and furrow, head on by a restored pond descending to a footbridge by an outcrop. Ignore the bridge, instead keep right in the dip following the fence to a hand-gate and confined path close by Newbrough Burn, emerge at a second hand-gate onto the road at the 30mph sign.

NEWBROUGH TO HALL BANK | >>

51 Go right up the road, the modern incarnation of the Stanegate – Roman engineers would be amazed by smooth rolled tarmacadam, how their chariots would have purred on such a surface! Take the first road right after crossing Settlingstones Burn, veer left at Stonecroft lodge on the lane to Bankfoot. Locate then cross the footbridge left, after the cottage adscend the pasture slope on a half-right diagonal line, cross a stile regaining the Stanegate road beside cottages. Continue over to the stile beside the large boulder, follow the field margin up to a gate into Fell Lane.

The rough tracked lane rises to the well-tended Fell Cottage, then winds higher to pass Fell House: all along enjoying truly wonderful views back over the South Tyne valley. Fell Lane gives out **49** onto a tarmac road at a green triangle, keep forward with the road through the hamlet of New Alston. Advance to the cross-roads, **48** turn right along North Road (named as from Haydon Bridge one presumes). Pass Cubstocks to reach Hall Bank **47** at the foot of the hill, turn left into Haresby Lonnen.

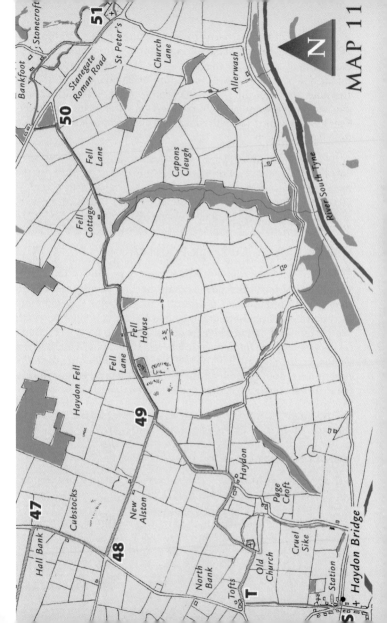

MAP 11

N

Bankfoot

Stonecroft

51

50

Stanegate Roman Road

St Peter's

Church Lane

Allerwash

Fell Lane

Capons Clough

River South Tyne

Fell Cottage

Fell House

Fell Lane

Haydon Fell

49

Cubstocks

Hall Bank

47

48

North Bank

New Alston

Tofts

T

Old Church

Haydon

Page Croft

Cruel Sike

Station

S

Haydon Bridge

River South Tyne

NEWBROUGH TO LAVERICK PLANTATION (12)
6.6 km | **4.1** miles > **2** hours

Should refreshment be an over-riding concern, wander on left into Newbrough (pronounced new-bruff), to patronise the Red Lion. Also pertinent: from here one may make a direct connection with the eastern end of the Moss Troopers' Trail (see page 118). Don't be deceived by the impressive Town Hall, this diminutive place is a village, a charming one too! The Mid Tyne Community Trust, formerly based next door, produced an excellent set of easy-to-follow country walk leaflets, the basis of numerous gentle days leisurely

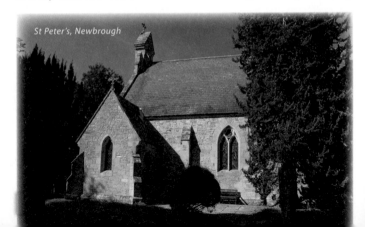

St Peter's, Newbrough

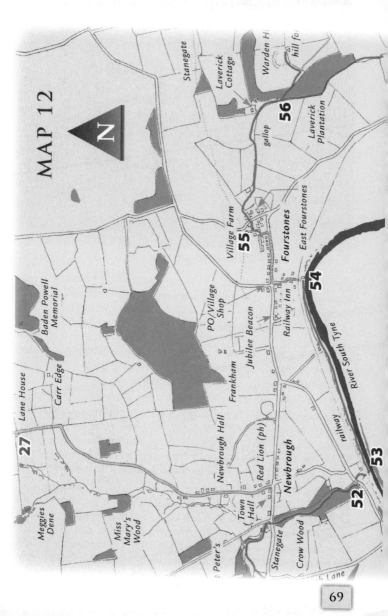

MAP 12

N

Meggies Dene

Miss Mary's Wood

Lane House

Carr Edge

Baden Powell Memorial

27

t Peter's

Town Hall

Newbrough Hall

Red Lion (ph)

Newbrough

Stanegate

Crow Wood

Lane

52

53

railway

River South Tyne

Frankham

Jubilee Beacon

PO/Village Shop

Railway Inn (ph)

Village Farm

55

Fourstones

East Fourstones

54

Stanegate

Laverick Cottage

Warden H

hill fo

56

gallop

Laverick Plantation

Fourstones from the bridlepath below Laverick Cottage

exploration of this area. However, The Roman Ring keeps faith with
Newbrough Burn crossing the road by the stone step-stile. Follow
the footpath signed 'Allerwash' leading on down through the lovely
Crow Wood, a popular local stroll. After crossing a footbridge and
coming close to a pasture fence, veer left from the weir to emerge
onto the B6319 – the mere fact that the road is numbered should
warn you to make sure your days are not numbered – and watch
both ways!

52 Turn left, proceed a matter of 40 metres, then turn right, into
the drive via a hand-gate signed 'Fourstones'. Coming close
to the cottage, bear right into the confined path leading down
steps under the railway, where the Newbrough Burn enters the
South Tyne. A coarse gravel path, hugging the left-hand side, gains
a level way beside the railway embankment, with splendid open
views of the river.

53 The riverside path comes as a lovely contrast to the recent
journey upon the higher pastures, with delightful scope for
waterside nature study. Where the wooded banks on the far bank
give way to eroded earthen banks note that this corresponds with
a litter of rocks in the river itself, washed out of the boulder clay.
The riverbank houses a substantial colony of sand martins. The

path is, at times, quite close to the river, and others are distanced by shingle and scrub; then it is tight by a fence through a wooded area, passing on by a lane-end cottage to reach Riverside Cottage, an impressively sited house.

54 Go left via the level-crossing – beware of trains – the penalty for not closing the gate 'a grand' giving you cause to comply. The roadway leads up by The Railway Inn to meet the village street facing St Aidan's Church, a diminutive green-painted timber building opposite the village shop. The road is again upon the line of The Stanegate. The village-name Fourstones refers to four lost stones that formed the core of a Bronze Age burial chamber. Ask a local what the name means and they'll offer a plausible explanation – the four stones quarried in the area, namely whinstone, limestone, sandstone and ganister (a form of leached sandstone located in beds close to coal measures), but of course this list fails to include the one commodity the community was wedded to, namely coal! Follow the footway right, where the semi-detached houses end cross by the new stone bus shelter. Go up the side road, locate a footpath signed 'Whinney Hill' right, immediately after 'The Gin Gan'. A confined path between gardens winds through, via hand-gates, by Village Farm Cottage to the road.

Chesters from Warden Hill

55 Go straight across, into the short lane between cottages to a stone step stile right of a field gate. Pass on by the cattle trough to the first gate right, festooned with barbed wire. Signpost 'Warden/Bridge End', pass through, and across the paddock joining the track above East Fourstones Farm. Go left passing through the gate, right of the dressage enclosure, ascending with a wall left and a horse gallop close right. A few metres short of the top of the second field go through the gate on the left passing gorse bushes to a wooden bridleway sign guiding up the track 'Warden'. A lovely view back down on Fourstones. The track leads to a gate by Laverick Cot-tage, a former gamekeeper's dwelling. Bear right, keeping the wall right, via a hand-gate beneath Laverick Plantation. The name Laverick refers to the skylark, the skies above Warden Hill will have long been associated with this most beautiful of songsters.

56 A bridleway sign 'Warden' directing left, spells an opportunity to consider a most pleasant spur path onto the top of Warden Hill. If this appeals, bear left, up through the mature conifers leaving the old sunken path to reach a bridle-gate. Turn right in the pasture to reach a gate in the corner, do not go through, instead ascend with the wall right onto the edge of the double ramparts of the Iron Age hill fort girdling Warden Hill. An Ordnance Survey column lurks through the ever-open gate right. The special view includes Sewingshields Farm on the north-west horizon; and Chesters House, the site of Cilurnum Roman Fort and the village of Wall, in the valley of the North Tyne to the north-east. The Romans will have wrested control of this native sanctuary to oversee their military way, The Stanegate, came up from Fourstones and dipped to a lost ford through the North Tyne then on towards Wall village. Retrace your steps back down through the plantation, regain the bridleway along the base of the woodland.

Continue south to emerge at a gate into pasture, advance to a watering place, go through the gate, putting the re-routed bridleway on the right-hand side of the hedge in a pasture that slopes away to the right. Down in the valley a constant hum, emitting from the Fourstones Paper Mill, and beyond the A69 only adding to the discord. Keep the hedge close left curving round to a gate, thereafter funnelling into a walled lane.

LAVERICK PLANTATION TO NEWBROUGH |>>

Continue to a hand-gate, now in the shelter of Laverick Plantation advance to a bridleway sign **56** where a spur path can be followed right ascending through the mature conifers to a hand-gate. At which point go right, at the field corner ignore the bridle-gate, bearing left up by the wall to gain the double ramparts of the Iron Age hill fort crowning Warden Hill – backtrack to continue. Pass through the next hand-gate to reach the track at Laverick Cottage, go through the gate left . Descend to an cluster of gorse bushes, and bridleway signpost directing left to the near gate. Continue the descent on the track, now with a wall right alongside a horse gallop. After the second gate pass the dressage enclosure, veering right across the paddock above East Fourstones Farm, to a gate and footpath sign. Turn left, via stile into a short lane flanked by cottages. **55** Cross the road via the hand-gate beside Village Farm Cottage, a confined path threads through between gardens to an estate road. Turn left by the entrance to The Gin Gan, to meet the main road. Turn right following the footway until opposite the green-painted timber-built St Aidan's Church, go left down the road signed for The Railway Inn. Pass on via the gated railway-crossing to stride respectfully across the lawn of Riverside Cottage, keep right **54**. The path now follows the riverbank of the South Tyne.

The path takes its leave of the railway embankment **53** sneaking under the railway bridge where Newbrough Burn enters the South Tyne. The path hugs the bridge wall, climbs steps and follows the confined path onto a drive that duly leads by a hand-gate onto the B6319 road. Turn left, walk some 40 metres to where a footpath is signed right via a hand-gate **52**. Follow Newbrough Burn upstream by a weir, then over a footbridge to emerge over a stone step-stile onto the road close to Newbrough. Go straight across via the facing hand-gate, keeping with the burn to a further hand-gate entering a pasture, head on to a footbridge, do not cross. Instead, veer left up the bank, to the left of a pond and fenced holy well, enter the churchyard via a wicket-gate. The path leads to the left of the church to reach a step-stile beside the lych-gate **51**.

LAVERICK PLANTATION TO TYNE GREEN (13)
5 km | **3.1** miles > **1.8** hours

57 After the wall-stile take the hand-gate right, descend the pasture with a fence close right. Go through the bridle-gate entering woodland to reach a cottage. Turn left following the confined footpath close to the railway to emerge at a lay-by.

58 *To the left St Michael's Church is well worth a visit with its 11th-century tower and unusual manacled graves — to prevent grave robbing. In the churchyard, find the Clayton family grave — John Clayton's name is hard to decipher under the moss.*

Follow the road right, passing under the railway bridge, to the Boatside Inn, renown for its fine fayre; note the the pub quoits team's site (to the left). Go straight across the road-bridge spanning the River South Tyne.

59 After the old toll cottage take the side road left, with Hadrian's Cycleway route 72 sign. Some 60 metres along the road watch for the sneaky start of the riverside path left by a gravel

St Michael's, Warden

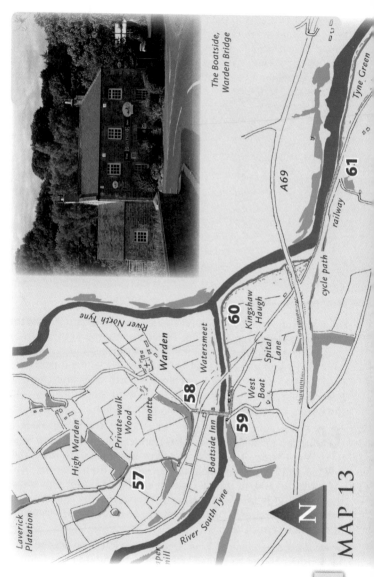

The Boatside, Warden Bridge

Laverick
Platation

High Warden

Private-walk
Wood

motte

River North Tyne

Warden

Watersmeet

57

58

Boatside Inn

59

West
Boat

Spital
Lane

60

Kingshaw
Haugh

A69

cycle path

railway

61

Tyne Green

River South Tyne

N

MAP 13

South Tyne from Warden Bridge

drive, with attendant decrepit Tyne Green Trail signboard. Follow the path along the sylvan riverbank. Passing under the slatted railway bridge witness the meeting of the rivers North and South Tyne. This spot can be said to be the origin of the name Tyne, 'the forked river' (the same as the 'tines' of a pitchfork – north tine, south tine). A popular pilgrimage for Tynesiders, the setting is impressively wild, the waters tumbling over a bouldery bed in union.

60 Follow along the flood bank, and, unless the river is exceptionally high, continue under the A69 road bridge. At times of flood, it is better to follow the cycle-path road from Warden Bridge, though a path can be pursued from the river right, via a kissing-gate, to connect with the cycle-path as it slips under the road bridge beside the railway. Keeping to the humble river path, weave through scrub to emerge onto the roadway beside the raised railway track, turn left.

61 As the parkland of Tyne Green opens left, bear off the road. Keep to the tree-lined riverside path through the Country

Park alongside the municipal golf course. The nineteen acres of meadow were given to the town by Wentworth Beaumont of Bywell Hall in 1887, though not quite the home-counties Wentworth, the sylvan park is greatly treasured and appreciatively used by the community. Built in 1793 Hexham Bridge forms the graceful end to this riverside passage. Beneath its arches is a weir impounding the river to give the allusion of a lake, the fine venue for a rowing club.

TYNE GREEN TO LAVERICK PLANTATION |>>

Follow the signs into the Tyne Green car park to bear right to the café **62** and the riverside walkway. Follow the path to where it meets the cycle path road beside the railway **61**. Turn right along the road tight beside the raised railway. Watch for the footpath, signed right, off the road to regain a wilder riverbank path leading under the A69 flyover and on by the flood-banking to the Tyne waters-meet **60**. The path becomes more confined by trees, again passing under the railway bridge to leave the riverbank left, via a short gravel drive re-join the cycleway on the side road.

Go right to the junction, turn right by the old toll cottage **59** and cross the South Tyne to The Boatside Inn. Branch onto the road to the right of the pub, passing under the railway again, at the lay-by on the left **58** locate a footpath signed left. The path, confined beside the railway, arrives at a cottage. Turn right in a woodland hollow-way rising to hand-gate. Ascend the pasture with a fence left to a hand-gate. Turn left via the wall-stile, the lane **57** funnelling out into a pasture. Keep to the top of the bank to a gate, continuing to a hand-gate, now in the shelter of Laverick Plantation.

TYNE GREEN TO PARK WOOD
4.5 km | **2.8** miles > **2** hours

(14)

62 Reaching the café, take leave of the riverbank, exiting the car park join the footway, cross the auction mart access road, to go right accompanying the main A6079 into town. Cross the railway, with the station on your left, and after the next roundabout bear left at the entrance to Morrisons. Walk through the large Wentworth car park, guided by the brown sign directing to the Tourist Information Centre. This is a stop for the AD 122 Roman Wall bus.

The Moothall, Hexham

63 Ascend the steps, of the pedestrian Hall Gate into the town centre. En route pass the imposing Manor Offices, built in 1332 as a prison for moss troopers and other local miscreants. It was probably originally linked by a curtain wall to the Moothall, a tower-house dating from the late 14th-century when it was a court and stronghold for the Archbishops of York. Go beneath the the Moothall's archway to enter the Market Place.

Across the beautiful Market Place from The Shambles stands Hexham Abbey. A visit is essential, the interior quite majestic, its stonework, fittings, carvings and panel paintings all of exceptional interest and quality. In the south transept, balanced against the wall, is a massive Roman tombstone from Corstopitum. Masonry from that site, and from the old Roman bridge at Corbridge, was used in much of the earliest building in AD 675 for Wilfred. The Crypt remains intact from this time and contains further Roman stone artefacts. The tombstone depicts Flavinus, standard-bearer of the Ala Petriana (present-day Stanwix in Carlisle) cavalry unit, bearing down upon a hapless native rebel. The stone symbolises

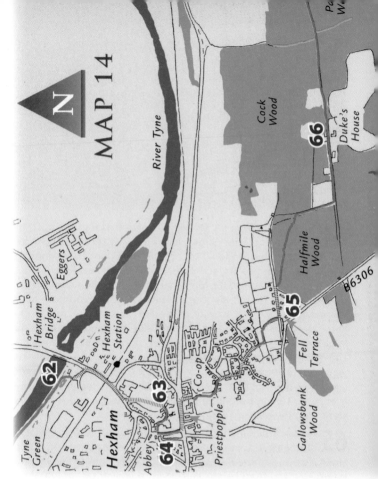

the honour of the ala, by his regalia and prancing mount. At his death Flavinus was 25 years old and had completed seven years service at Corstopitum. One interesting observation is the mix of sandstone used in the construction of the abbey itself: in the north transept the red crumbly masonry is out of kilter with the rest of the fabric, it would appear to be Cumbrian, possibly from the Gelt quarries near Brampton.

Hexham Abbey

64 From The Shambles follow the pedestrian shopping thoroughfare of Fore Street left into Priestpopple. Turn left passing a small bus station, turn right at the County Hotel into the side street of Argyle Terrace. Pass the NFU offices of Agriculture House to reach the new Co-op supermarket, on the site of the old Livestock Mart. Go left via the zebra crossing, then right, through the car park onto a footway and steps, leading left up to the housing estate. Coming along Allen Drive by the entrance to the Middle School gain Wanless Lane. Keep right into Bondgate Close and straight on into Greenbank, seeking a footpath sign 'Fellside' via two short flights of steps above garden fencing. At the second lamp bear half-right, off the tarmac path up the rough bank on a narrow trod path, becoming confined by a hedge and fencing, to steps onto the road at Fellside terrace.

65 A good moment to pause and glance back over Hexham, to a distant north-west horizon sighting of Sewingshields Crags and the course of the Roman Wall, and closer right in the vale the steam emitting from Eggers cardboard pulpworks. Turn left along the road to a turning area, follow a footpath signed right 'Dukes House'. A lovely sylvan way uphill, with waymark posts ensuring you hold to the main path through Halfmile Wood. On reaching a fenced paddock is notice the woodant hills, composed of pine needle debris near right. Advance to meet a broad track from the Blanchland road. Go left, signed 'Dilston' to pass the impressive Dukes House.

Hexham from Fellside

PARK WOOD TO TYNE GREEN |>>

The woodland path follows a low banking, then after a signpost becoming a broader track leading on past the Dukes House. The woodland drive leads on past the impressive Dukes House **66** (destination the Blanchland road). However, at the end of a paddock follow a footpath, signed right, by the paddock fence into Halfmile Wood. Descend to a road, go left finding another footpath sign right, at the beginning of Fellside terrace **65**, with its splendid view over Hexham. Descend steps, now confined between a fence and hedge, dip down a rough bank onto a tarmac path at the rear of an estate of modern houses. Follow this left into Greenbank, Bondgate Close then Wanless Drive and Allen Drive passing on down through the Co-op car park into Argyle Terrace. Continue via the zebra crossing, to enter Priestpopple by the County Hotel, turn left then right into Fore Street to reach the Market Place **64**. Go right, through the Moothall's arch, descend Hall Garth to the TIC **63** at the edge of the Wentworth car park. Traverse the car park to the left of Morrisons crossing, follow the footway alongside the main road, cross the railway. Follow the signs into the Tyne Green car park, bear right to the café **62** and the riverside walkway.

66 Pass Dukes House, an impressive building, now a private residence but for a time was a school. Built in 1873 as a country residence for John Backhouse, a Sunderland industrialist, his town house now absorbed into Sunderland University's campus. Dukes House was the only domestic indulgence of architect Frank Caws, a Gothic feast bristling with devices and at least 35 chimneys. Caws designed the opulent interior for the cruise-liner Mauretania, built at Swan Hunters' shipyard, plumb on the eastern extremity of the Roman Wall, at Wallsend. The house-name derives from the Duke of Somerset of Raglan Castle, who was captured at the battle of Hexham Levels in 1484, during the Wars of the Roses. He was taken to Hexham Market Place, beheaded and his head borne south for public exhibition on London Bridge. The track dwindles after two path junctions, signed 'Dilston', becoming little more than a woodland path beside a low bank in Dilston Park Wood. This leads into a narrow tree-lined passage between arable fields, the early stile, by boulders, installed as part of commendable environmental stewardship access (see the information panel). Lower down, the path can be prone to entanglement with briars and nettles.

67 Emerging into a farm lane at a gate, go straight ahead, down the green lane to a cottage and subsequent gate. Now becoming a confined path, with a scout campsite meadow right. A red-painted Shino tori gate draws eyes left, over a field-gate into the Dilston Physic Garden. The garden is only open from April to September, for two hours a week each Wednesday, but will appeal to those with an interest in herbalism and alternative healing. It contains an array of culinary areas, a camomile lawn; an area for the heart and mind, a bamboo avenue and in excess of 500 medical plants that form the basis of health, and restorative cures. The path leads onto the track by Dilston Mill following the access lane beside Devils Water to the main road A695. To the south lies Dilston Hall, now a college for those of 'differing abilities'; there is an excellent café run by the students. Dilston was the seat of the Earls of Derwentwater, Northumbrian Jacobites. For those with the

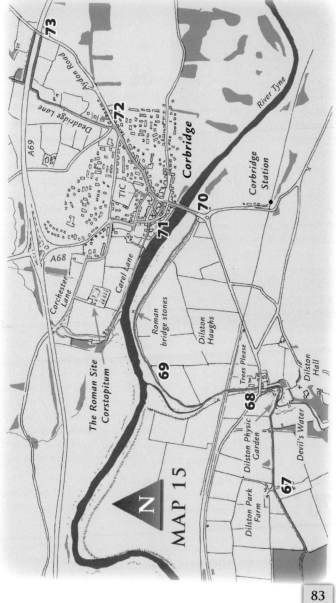

MAP 15

N

73

72

Corbridge

River Tyne

Corbridge Station

70

71

TIC

A69

Lydon Road

Deadridge Lane

A68

Corchester Lane

Carel Lane

The Roman Site
Corstopitum

Roman
bridge stones

Dilston Haughs

69

Trees Please

68

Dilston
Hall

Devil's Water

Dilston Physic
Garden

Dilston Park
Farm

67

time, the restored Chapel is worth a visit.

68 Turn right, crossing the footway over the bridge. A footpath sign beside the sheds of 'Trees Please' indicates left to 'Corbridge'. Step down, through the kissing-gate to a confined path, leading to hand-gates on either side of the busy railway. For all the good visibility of the long straight track – take care in stepping over the lines. The path now continues with a wall right, downstream with Devils Water to its confluence with the River Tyne.

69 Keep beside the Tyne on Dilston Haughs to reach a gathering of large tooled stones (left). These were excavated from the site of the Roman Corstopitum bridge which carried Dere Street into the Roman town. It was the largest bridge in Roman Britain, some ten piers wide, greater than Chesters or Pons Aelius (Newcastle). Footings from the triumphal arch have been found – though it should be pointed out that the river drifted south since Roman times, so strictly these stones are on the wrong bank! Join the recently restored flood-bank to reach a kissing-gate onto the road beside lights controlling traffic over the Tyne Bridge.

70 Follow the footway over the bridge to enter Corbridge. Rising into Broad Street turn left from Barclays Bank along Fore Street into the Market Place.

71 There is are an abundance of places for refined and casual refreshment in this, the smartest of country town destinations.

Inspect St Andrew's Church, notice the 14th-century King's Oven in the boundary wall; remaining from a time when dough was taxed. The Vicar's Pele (currently empty), was built around 1300 from Roman stones filched from Corstopitum; desparate times when the priest was as exposed as anyone to attack.

No visit to this town is remotely complete without inspecting the Roman remains. Either follow the Carel Gate, (meaning 'the road to Carlisle' – and an alternative name for Stanegate), via Well Lane or stay by the road via Watling Street (misnamed, it is really part of the Roman Dere Street) and the footway beside Corchester Lane to reach the English Heritage site. The actual Roman town spread over an area of 24 acres but only two acres (seven percent) are exposed close to the museum. They are fascinating remains and the museum itself a place of inspirational quest. Corstopitum was a strategic military town, at the eastern end of Stanegate, the pre-Hadrian's Wall frontier road from Carlisle (Luguvalium), built by Agricola. Dere Street ran south from here to York (Eboricum), the legionary administrative headquarters for northern Britannia, continuing north via Portgate, where there was a major frontier gate later when the the Wall was imposed.

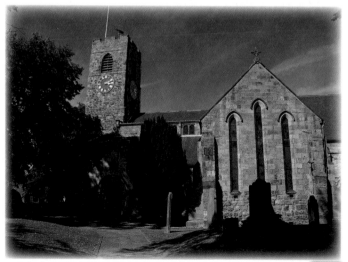

St Andrews, Corbridge

Follow the passage beside the Vicar's Pele into Hill Street. Keep right to the Tourist Information Centre, turning left by the Golden Lion into Princess Street. The Golden Lion was built from stones recycled from Dilston Hall, home of the aforementioned Jacobite, not as it says on the wall plaque a 'Jockobite' — though this might amuse any passing Scot! Walk up the footway noting the horse watering troughs right, and later, to the left the Victorian Post Box on the Coach House. Opposite the Northumbria Police building, at the entrance to a house called 'Riversdale', take a left turn, choose the right-hand of two lanes, Deadridge Lane.

DEADRIDGE LANE TO PARK WOOD | >>

Deadridge Lane merges with Milkwell Lane, joins the Aydon Road **72** then leads down the footway into Corbridge becoming Princess Street. Turn right along Hill Street by the TIC, bear left by the churchyard wall to the Vicar's Pele **71**. *Do make time to visit the remains of the Roman town of Corstopitum — reach the Roman Site either by following the footways along Watling Street and Corchester Lane, or from the river bridge along the Carel Gate foo tpath.*

The main route leaves the Market Place left along Fore Street to Broad Street. Turn right to cross the Tyne bridge, and at the traffic lights go right **70** via the kissing-gate onto the flood-banking. Follow this to the fenced off collection of stones excavated from the Roman bridge that carried Dere Street into the Roman town. Continue with the riverside meadow along Dilston Haughs, from the waters-meet **69** follow Devils Water upstream. Cross the railway cautiously via facing hand-gates. Advance to a kissing-gate and steps up onto the road by the plant nursery 'Trees Please'. Take the footway over the bridge **68** bearing left into the lane to Dilston Mill signed 'Herbs for Health and Healing'. Continue up the green path by the Physic Garden, to a cottage and gate. Keep in the green lane, crossing a farm track at Dilston Park then **67** via a gate into a more confined passage rising between arable fields to enter Park Wood.

Aydon Castle

72 A bridleway sign directs 'Aydon Road', higher up Deadridge Lane the road becomes a bridlepath. But just before it does notice the two beehive brick pottery kilns away to the left. Coming alongside the fencing of the A69 the passage duly emerges onto Aydon Road at a hand-gate.

73 Turn left over the flyover by the barriers to enter the bridleway once more, immediately left at a hand-gate signed 'Aydon Castle'. A fenced passage heads west to regain the original line of the bridleway, so rudely interrupted by construction of the A69. The confined path veers right up to a recessed hand-gate, presumably to allow horse-riders to dismount. Head north with a wall, then fence, to a bridle-gate on the right at the ridge top, go through and curve naturally around the shallow combe in the pasture to enter the mature larch woodland at a bridle-gate.

The old pathway leads down through the woodland strip to a small footbridge over Cor Burn, look for the bright rust-red boggy 'flushes' where iron oxides are precipitated from the spring-waters as they meet the atmosphere – this was an early source of iron. Climb the steep woodland path to a hand-gate left of Aydon Castle's curtain walls (English Heritage).

74 There can be no denying the romance of the setting, and the interest in the building. With good reason considered the finest castellated manor house in England, defensive medieval domesticity. Do give it your avid attention, it's time very well spent. Some walkers with 'long-in-the-tooth' memories by recall the fictional medieval television tales of 'Ivanhoe': this off-the-beaten-track site proved the perfect film location for the series.

The route goes through the gate and past the entrance to join the minor road – it is tarmac the remainder of the way to Onnum Roman Fort, though thankfully these are quiet country roads. Past the castle car park, and on to the next road junction with the road sign 'Halton'. Follow this right, there is a fine view of Halton Tower at the end of a beautifully tended formal lawn.

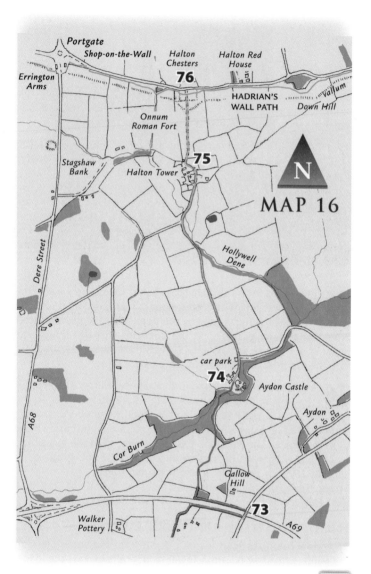

Halton Tower

75 Pay a visit to the church, this affords a close-up view of the pele tower element of this elegantly proportioned fortified house. Follow the private road by the pond, walkers only welcome. From the cottage progress up the unenclosed road through the midst of pasture. A rampart heralds the site of Halton Chesters Wall fort, the irregular banks secreting raw archaeology.

76 At the stone piers, giving onto the busy Military Road B6318, The Roman Ring is re-united with the National Trail. To the east, spot the corrugated profile of the Wall vallum on Down Hill; composed of limestone, the hill is a glacial raft shifted three miles from the north. The National Trail heads west from the fort site to reach the Errington Arms (being restored after a catastrophic fire early in 2006) at Portgate, a major Roman frontier gate on Dere Street, their principal military road, close to the site of Stagshaw Bank Fair, at one time the largest drovers' market in England.

HALTON CHESTERS TO DEADRIDGE LANE | >>

76 Follow the open road leading down from the stone piers off the Military Road with Halton Tower in view ahead. Pass the lodge,

Approaching Halton Chesters

keeping with the road as it veers left, down past the church **75** then on to the minor road junction. Keep left, signed to Aydon Castle. Pass the English Heritage car park to approach the high curtain wall of Aydon Castle **74** via a gate, to a bridle-gate. Dip into the wooded dell on an old pathway, to a small footbridge over Cor Burn. Continue up the modified hollow-way path, through the larch plantation to emerge at a bridle-gate into a large pasture. Naturally follow the curve of the combe round to a bridle-gate on the top of the ridge. Turn left gently descending by the fence, then wall, to a protecting fenced bridle-gate, enter a confined pathway. The imposition of the A69 has caused the path to switch left to a hand-gate **73** follow the barriers right, over the road bridge to regain the modified bridle-path at the hand-gate. Continuing as a fenced passage the bridleway duly bears away from the noisy road into a Deadridge Lane, becoming a quiet by-road on course to reach the foot of Milkwell Lane and the Aydon Road into Corbridge.

MOSS TROOPERS' TRAIL

Carvoran to Newbrough

32 km | **20** miles > **2** days

A PATH FOR FAIR SEASONS

dreamers, drovers, reivers and rogues

The Roman Wall faces north over a sparsely populated countryside, dotted with farmsteads and backed by the lost horizons of the Border Forests. This is a landscape over which people have gazed and travelled down the ages. Cattle drovers and Tynedale traders in the main, even in Roman times, when there was much trade through the milecastle gates. In medieval times there were raiding brigands and rogues who found sanctuary in this moorland wilderness, long before the advent of the conifer forestry. King's Wicket between Housesteads and Sewingshields is traditionally known as Busy Gap from this activity, hence the Busy Gap Rogue. Yet there will always be a sense of romance in this wild land and in the perspectives it gives back upon the Wall.

The Moss Troopers' Trail beckons. Leading immediately north from the environs of Carvoran and Walltown Quarry, it sets course eastward, parallel with the Whin Sill, seldom more than a mile or so north from the Wall all the way to Simonburn, reuniting with the Wall then stepping over into Tynedale to end at Newbrough.

Always on this journey the eyes will be trained southward to the line of scarps that form the centrepiece of the frontier. This is a walking quest that will intrigue by revealing another dimension on these scarplands, a telling trail in a wilder territory.

This is a land that had lain beyond the Roman Empire, though never outside its forceful influence. Contemporary Latin chroniclers referred to the natives as bearded barbarians, and many of their descendants live here today. I may cite the tenant of West Stonefolds (east of Greenlee Lough) who has the surname 'Waugh'; the Vikings, while colonising the area, referred to the native folk as 'waughs'. A thousand years on, and the Border Reiving Moss Trooper called

Ruined shieling beside the Black Dyke, marking the eastern edge of Wark Forest

an unsavoury tune, rustling cattle and pillaging farms, their roguish activities leading them north and south, east and west across its troubled land. And for centuries betwix and between, farmers have sought to eke out a living as stockmen in an unforgiving climate harangued by icy winds and rain. To casual eyes this is a bleak landscape of rush pasture and mossy mire, from which the sombre misty lost horizons of the Border forests fade into a distant haze. But the vision of the mind ignites when in contact with this forgotten world. Removed from encounters with the casual tourist, this is the Wall country that the wandering spirit will adore.

The Nine Nicks of Thirlwall form a dramatic western flourish to the Whin Sill upon which rests an eye-catching exhibition of the Hadrian's Wall monument. The Roman Army Museum at Carvoran, close to the site of Magnis, is well worth visiting. Magnis Roman fort pre-dates the Wall itself, lying at the junction of the east/west Stanegate and the southward Pennine traversing Maiden Way.

Many visitors casually visit the Walltown Quarry Picnic Site with its grand exposure of dolerite, a very hard basalt otherwise known by its Northumbrian name Whin Sill. Beyond, visitors are drawn up to Hadrian's Wall Path onto the edge of Walltown Crags to witness the delightful twists and turns of the consolidated Roman Wall along this famous section of scarp to the Roman signal station.

For the more determined, the National Trail runs on east by a series of thrilling moments over Mucklebank Crag to Great Chesters, followed by a memorable sequence of startling craggy rims – Cawfields, Winshields, Peel, Highshields, and Hotbank on course for Housesteads, and later still Sewingshields Crags: without question stirring stuff. But for all the genuine thrills such a succession provides, the Roman frontier was as broad as it was long. To know the historic lay of the land, to see the area as the Romans themselves knew it, patrolling north on sorties to their outpost forts, whether on charm offences or in crushing tribal insurrections: enter the lonesome land of the Moss Trooper – stick tightly to the narrow line of the Wall itself, for the 'blinkered' view.

CARVORAN TO BUNDLE HILL (17)
4 km | **2.5** miles > **1.3** hours

Leave the National Trail on the minor road at grid ref 668661. This is the point where Hadrian's Wall Path begins its plunge down the banks beside the lost Wall's north ditch to Thirlwall Castle, bound for the Tyne Gap, Gilsland and entry into Cumbria. Looking westward you get a distant tantalising glimpse of the Solway Firth backed by the Dumfries hill, Criffel – most picturesque as the evening throws a ribbon of silvery light onto the estuary.

1 Follow the minor road north crossing two cattle-grids. The single-track road has passing places and ample verges for off tarmac walking. The caution to 'Slow down young lambs on road' confirms this to be sheep-rearing country, though there is no shortage of cattle either, humans the rarer animal! The road briefly dips, to the right – an interesting profile of old man, this is Collar Heugh Crag. One wonders how each generation has considered this craggy face. Is it a Roman nose you see? The name is intriguing in itself, does it refer to someone called Heugh dressed up in a starched collar? The farm-name 'shield' is from the Viking (shiel) and refers to a summer farmstead. After the next left turn in the road notice a solitary boulder close to the fence, composed of quartz, this is an erratic carried by ice all the way from the Lake District!

MAP 17

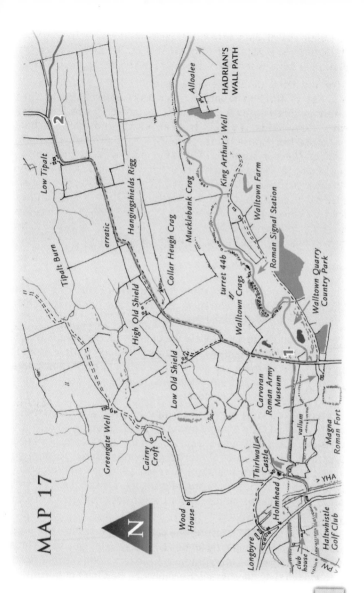

HADRIAN'S WALL PATH

Alloalee

Low Tipalt

Tipalt Burn

Hangingshields Rigg

erratic

Collar Heugh Crag

Mucklebank Crag

King Arthur's Well

Walltown Farm

Roman Signal Station

turret 44b

Walltown Crags

Walltown Quarry Country Park

High Old Shield

Low Old Shield

Carvoran Roman Army Museum

Greengate Well

Cairny Croft

Wood House

vallum

Magna Roman Fort

Thirlwall Castle

Holmhead

YHA

Longbyre

club house

Haltwhistle Golf Club

Md

N

Open road leading past Collar Heugh Crag

The road dips off Hangingstone Rigg, down a bank towards Low Tipalt. Pass the farm entrance, advance to a bridleway signing straight ahead, as the road bears left.

2 Go through the gate, follow the open track. Heed the waymark post, this guides off the track onto the rough pasture, leading to a gate set in the fence some 60 yards south of the track gate. Watch your footing in front of the gate, beware the ditch – draining from a dyke in the next enclosure.

Entering Access Land, veer half right to traverse a broad mossy shelf, a modest taste of moss tramping, if not trooping! Aim for the dry slope some 250 metres away, follow this to a waymark sleeper post and adjacent pair of stones gate posts. Don't go through, keep the zig-zagging wall right, to reach a new galvanised gate on Bundle Hill. Advance eastward, reasonably close to the wall, with only cattle tracks as guide, later a tractor track suffices to reach a gate and subsequent open road.

One may turn right, crossing the cattle grid and follow the road, via Burnhead Moss, directly to the Wall at Cawfields Quarry in a little over a mile. However, Moss Troopers head left, along the road north – as indeed they may have done in history, evading hot pursuit!

MAP 18

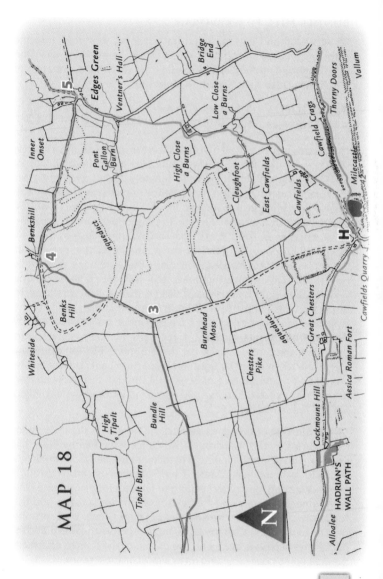

Pass through and join the open track leading to a gate onto the road **2**. Continue west passing Low Tipalt Farm rising onto the rigg, keeping faithfully to the road all the way to the entrance to **1** Walltown Quarry and Carvoran Museum.

BUNDLE HILL TO EDGES GREEN

(18)

4 km | **2.5** miles > **1.3** hours

3 Passing a decrepit rail freight wagon the road dips into a hollow. The causeway at the foot was built over the contouring loop of the Aesica Roman aqueduct. Unfortunately, rushes and long grass obscure the narrow cut but its existence has been verified through careful archaeological investigation. A hint to its course will be spotted shortly at Edges Green. The aqueduct ran an amazing seven miles from Fond Tom's Pool in Caw Burn close to Swallow Crags, falling on a tiny gradient to supply the Roman garrison at Great Chesters (Aesica). Smart cookies these Romans they knew how to do civil engineering, make that military engineering. The very existence of this aqueduct indicates that the land to the north of the Wall was not overtly hostile, at least not in the vicinity of the Wall, for Aesica fort could not have depended on its water supply coming from hostile territory. A footpath sign shows two paths diverging, the more obvious on the ground is not for us; follow 'Benkshill 0.5', in effect straight up the pasture bank, traversing the undulating rough pasture of Benks Hill through a shallow hollow, to regain the road (of course you may simply follow the encircling road to the same effect).

4 Stepping over the roadside ditch go right with the open road, ignore the northward track, which leads by nearby Benkshill Cottage – on course for lonely Scotchcoulthard; derived from 'Scot's colt herd' meaning horses stolen from Scotland. Instead, go through the poorly hung road gate, keeping to tarmac along a winding lane with some young trees planted close by. Crossing a cattle-grid the road draws close to the little hamlet of Edges Green. Look into the pasture to the right, after some 200 metres, before the wall draws in, note a line of rushes betraying the course of the Roman aqueduct; the little pump house standing on its almost invisible course.

Gibbs Hill

EDGES GREEN TO BUNDLE HILL |>>

5 Cross the grid then bear right over the road bridge. Keep with the tarmac road via two further cattle-grids to reach a poorly hung road gate **4**. March on to the second telegraph pole before hopping over the roadside ditch and to ascend the open pasture traversing Benks Hill. Re-join the road where two paths converge. Ascend the open road passing the old wagon to reach a cattle-grid. **3** Bear off onto the pasture, before the grid bridleway sign 'Low Tipalt'. Advance to a new wooden gate in a fence after some 150 metres, continue upon an often damp greenway with a wall left to a galvanised gate in a fence on Bundle Hill. Follow on, through rushy pasture, with the remains of a wall zig-zagging close left. At the enclosure corner, stone posts stand beside a waymarked sleeper in the mire, continue west keeping to the lower slopes of the bank. After some 400 metres bear half-right following an open ditch to a gate in the fence.

EDGES GREEN TO GREENLEE FARM-TRACK (19)
5.1 km | **3.2** miles > **1.8** hours

5 Cross the road bridge, bear left over the grid by Edges Green Farm. Ignore the road right, hold to the open road heading north-east passing over the brow, and on via a further grid coming close to the edge of Herding Crags. Appropriately, cattle still congress upon this shallow scarp, the odd wedged standing stone adding to the curiosity value of a moment's pause. The outlook is extensive and wild, made all the more remote by the middle distance onset of forestry. The road is motorable – through to Wark in North Tynedale.

6 Leave the firm comfort of the unenclosed road, where a footpath sign 'Melkridge Common' is spotted a matter of 20 metres to the right beside an enclosure access gate. Keeping the wall close left advance through the pathless, rushy pasture, latterly by a corner enclosure defined by a fence, to a ladder-stile set in a boggy hollow. This rather nondescript place is Resting Gap. The name, the clue to its former strategic importance, cattle drovers primarily will have used it to 'hold over' on their long drifts too and fro the Tyne valley and Stagshaw Fair; the name Watch Hill indicates the concern for ambush from moss troopers. That border reivers too may have brought their ill-gotten gains this way is for ever likely, the fold in the hill the perfect temporary hideaway from hot-foot pursuers. Drift half-right, away from the wall, crossing over the dry pasture of Watch Hill. Passing a cluster of boulders and through a wireless fenceline, head through the rougher pasture towards a solitary tree. This concludes at a ladder-stile close to Wealside Farm.

7 Intriguingly the farm-name Wealside would appear to mean 'the welshman's pasture', a rare echo from the pre-Anglian settlement of this area. Set in the pasture a little to the north of the farmyard, is a raptor roost used in the rearing of falcons. Please note the farmyard is not a right-of-way, so there is no connection with the apparent county road to Edges Green. Turn abruptly left beside the wall, as the grassy track ends bear half-right across the dry pasture to a ladder-stile entering Access Land. Keep the wall close right and pass a newly restored sheepfold set into the wall. Cross a ladder-stile into a broad, short drove lane; the broken edge of Swallow Crags catches attention over to the right. Note the track ramp in its midst this leads over the rigg to ford Caw Burn, just downstream of Fond Tom's Pool (mentioned in **3** above). The lane ends at a stile and gateway. Rough pasture ensues due east, aim for the covered yard in the distance, at Gibbs Hill, there is poor evidence of a path – other than that made by loafing cattle. Cross the ladder-stile, a tractor track comes to the rescue! Follow this track, avoiding the

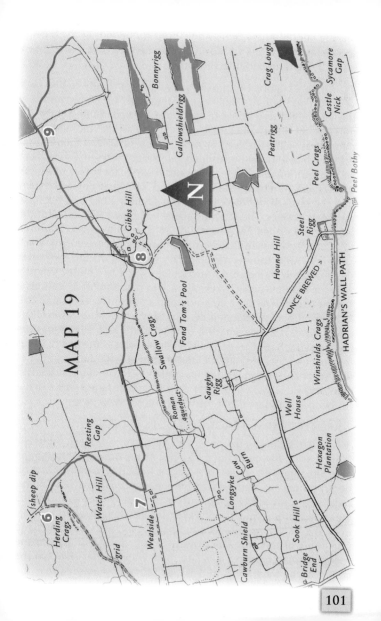

MAP 19

Bonnyrigg

Gallowshieldrigg

Crag Lough

Sycamore Gap

Castle Nick

Peatrigg

Peel Crags

Peel Bothy

9

N

Gibbs Hill

Steel Rigg

8

Hound Hill

Swallow Crags

Fond Tom's Pool

ONCE BREWED

Roman aqueduct

Saughy Rigg

Winshields Crags

HADRIAN'S WALL PATH

Resting Gap

Watch Hill

Well House

Longsyke

Caw Burn

Hexagon Plantation

sheep dip

6

Herding Crags

7

Wealside

Cawburn Shield

Sook Hill

Bridge End

grid

marshy mire of Allery Burn. Angle right to the foot of the bank at the eastern end of the Swallow Crags scarp, then continue to a gate into a fenced lane at Gibbs Hill Farm.

9 Arrival at Gibbs Hill provides a solid opportunity to link back south to Hadrian's Wall Path at Steel Rigg (1.75 miles) and over the Whin Sill ridge down to the Once Brewed Youth Hostel (2.5 miles) – all upon minor roads. But it should not be overlooked that Gibbs Hill Farm itself provides excellent accommodation for walkers, including a twenty-bed bunkhouse. The first farm here was only a summer abode, it was not a safe place to live, the cruel winters only part of the threat to life and limb. Heed not the hearsay that the farm-name refers to a sheep stealers gibbet, as the local term was gallows. The Moss Troopers' Trail now bears left with the fenced track signed 'East Stonefolds 2.5'. The notice draws attention to a long-established Countryside Stewardship agreement, which includes a wild country circular walk sweeping off the track over the near horizon including the boulder waste of Chatley Crags: a walk for the lone spirit, tracking back in time too for it features a Bronze Age funeral cairn centred upon an orthostat capping a cist. Passing a pond surrounded by a nursery of deciduous trees, the track opens at a gate and runs unfettered through a large pasture field to a gate/ladder-stile. The view back features Winshields Crags framing the distant Cold Fell, northernmost 2,000 foot summit of the Pennines, Denton Fell and Mucklebank Crag on the Wall leading to Walltown Crags. Continuing with the open farm track reach a further gate/ladder-stile at the very corner of Wark Forest.

GREENLEE FARM-TRACK TO EDGES GREEN |>>

9 Turn left, following the open track via gates to arrive at Gibbs Hill farm. Passing the pond the track rises. At the brow go through the gate left signed 'Wealside' **8**. A tractor track degenerates, through boggy ground, to a ladder-stile. Here, evidence of a path is minimal; traverse a comparably damp pasture to a pile of rubble, and broad gateway, entry into a short walled lane ending in a ladder-stile. Keep the wall close left, now on firm pasture, with just one damp ford short of the next ladder-stile. Bear half-right in dry pasture to join, and accompany, a wall to the inviting ladder-stile **7** in the corner of the field, short of Wealside farmyard. Please note – the

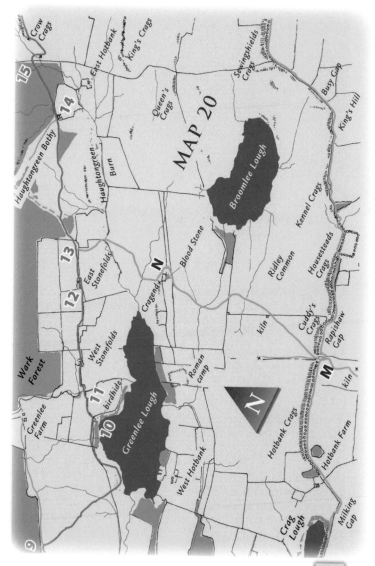

Boardwalk at Greenlee Lough

farmyard is not a right-of-way, so the continuing county road to Edges Green cannot be joined from here. Guided by the footpath sign, angle half-right up the rough pasture, first by an open ditch, then pathless to reach the dry pasture of Watch Hill. Continue via a cluster of boulders, through a wireless fence, slipping over the ridge to a ladder stile in the boggy hollow of Resting Gap. Continue with the fence, then wall, close right to meet the open road. **6** Turn left following the road over Herding Crags and down by a cattle grid to the hamlet of Edges Green **5**.

GREENLEE FARM-TRACK TO HAUGHTON GREEN (20)
4 km | **2.5** miles > **1.3** hours

9 Follow the track for a matter of 150 metres to where a footpath sign directs half-right to 'Greenlee Lough and bird-hide'. Here Moss Troopers' join the Greenlee Lough Trail, established after the Northumberland National Park Authority (in association with English Nature (now Natural England), the Heritage Memorial Fund and the Northumberland Wildlife Trust) acquired the precious farm, fen and open water estate in 1991. Traverse the rushy pasture via intermediate waymark posts to reach a hand-gate in a fence. Go

Birdhide at Greenlee Lough

through, step onto the boardwalk. Whether high or low water, the boardwalk ensures minimal visitor impact on the sphagnum fen. So, keep on the walkway, there's no knowing how far you'll be sucked in! The boardwalk makes no contact with the open water, but the immediate flora and potential fauna more than compensate. Take especial care in wet weather and winter: this boardwalk can be very slippery. A quiet demeanour is advised, a noisy approach can scare the birds from the lake, spoiling the viewing from the hide. Visitors should obtain the special leaflet prepared by the Park Authority (copies are often to be found in the bird-hide), of even more importance – a pair of binoculars – indispensable. The sighting of playful otter, one of the extra special treats of any visit. The boardwalk curves back to the fence and ends. Step off keeping the fence close left, muddy ground inevitable, advance to a ladder-stile crossing a wall. A fenced enclosure fostering a diverse collection of native trees means that the trail is ousted left, over the stile and into a pasture field. Keep the fence right, to a stile short of the next wall, enter the loughside enclosure access to the bird-hide.

10 Approach with stealth, unfortunately the entrance door is open to the lough, it would be better at the back to enable you to sneak inside and get surprise sightings. Heron are notoriously flighty, the resident swans and mallard tend to congregate on the far bank, but there's plenty of scope to enjoy good spotting sessions, be prepared to give time to the process. For all that the lough is little more than seven feet deep at best, the mire would soon consume anyone who wanders out into it's midst: be warned!

It is hard to over-estimate the importance of the richness of the habitat of Northumberland's largest natural lake. The fringing fen harbours many rare species, hence its designation as a National Nature Reserve. In winter, look for visiting whooper swans, distinguished from the resident mute swans by their gentle yellow and black bills. Notice also the elegant goosander, and duck such as wigeon and teal. Ocassionally, in spring and autumn, a passing osprey stops off at the lough for refuelling. Stepping back over the stile, turn right keeping the field wall close right to a three-way sign.

11 Take the path signed 'East Stonefolds 0.75' straight ahead, skirt a patch of nettles to a stile/gate. A passage beside a small plantation leads down to a ladder-stile and footbridge over

Greenlee Burn. The path draws up leftwards to a wall corner, and follows the wall directly to West Stonefolds. Ideally, the path would continue on the north side of the property, but at present the right-of-way is ushered over a ladder-stile and in front of the house – respect the owner's privacy as you pass his front door, to reach the gate, follow the open access track is to East Stonefolds.

12 Cross the ladder-stile,proceed past the stone barns and East Stonefolds farmhouse, no longer functioning as an agricultural holding, but obviously a much-loved home to judge from the order in the flower and vegetable gardens. The ensuing track duly merges with the Pennine Way.

13 This is the last moment for walkers to consider linking back south towards Hadrian's Wall; via Rapishaw Gap (1.4 miles) or via the continuing footpath across the Vallum, make a link with The Roman Ring (2.2 miles) at Crindledykes.

The track leads to a ladder-stile/gate entering Wark Forest. The mercy is that our trail gives the enormous conifer entanglement the briefest of brushes. A sign 'Haughton Green 0.5' after some 220 metres directs right, off the hardcore track onto a trimmed green way. The original forest planting has been felled, the views restored to the attractive heather and craggy scarps that lay, near south,

Haughtongreen Bothy

The brief walk through Wark Forest

towards the Whin Sill. The path leads on to a lonesome cottage of some antiquity, Haughton Green Bothy. Maintained by the Mountain Bothies Association for small-scale occupancy by all lovers of wild places: the perfect haven for hard-pressed hikers, be they Pennine Wayfarers or contemporary Moss Troopers. The property lies on a cattle drove (or drift) from Scotland, coming east from Robinrock bound for the age-old open-air cattle fair at Stagshaw Bank, situated close to eastern limit of Hadrian's Wall Conservation Corridor at Halton Chesters.

HAUGHTON GREEN TO GREENLEE FARM-TRACK |>>

The confined path through the conifers is mercifully short, quickly a burn intervenes - the best way to cross? Dodging into the trees left before re-gaining the sunlit green ribbon. Latterly wind-blown trees have smothered the path, again dodged by dipping left to cross a small hand-railed footbridge emerging beside the bounding wall. Keep right, take the left fork path signed to 'Stonefolds', pass Haughtongreen Bothy **14**. The broad swath of path leads to a forestry track meeting the Pennine Way. Turn left to leave Wark Forest via a gate. **13** Keep with the track, leading through East Stonefolds via gates **12** continuing to West Stonefolds. Enter by a gate (loose dog notice), and exit over a ladder-stile. Advance with the wall left, to dip to a footbridge and ladder-stile adjacent to a belt of woodland. Proceed to a three-way sign, **11** go forward, signed 'birdhide' wending down the pasture's edge to reach a stile giving access to the birdhide **10**. The route continues right, to a stile in the field corner, and promptly crosses the ladder-stile. Follow the fence west onto the boardwalk, which curves through the wetland fringe and then back to a gate in the bounding fence. A narrow path ascends the rushy pasture via three waymark posts to meet the Greenlee Farm access track beside the forest **9**.

HAUGHTON GREEN TO GREAT LONBROUGH (21)
4 km | 2.5 miles > **1.5** hours

14 The next stage in the journey may begin cramped by glowering conifers but soon opens to wide horizons, beyond the forest bounds traversing an undulating rushy prairie grazed by cattle and sheep. A three-way sign indicates 'Great Lonbrough 2.5' straight ahead with the wall right, and forest left. The comfort zone of the wall is lost as the path pitches half-left to a simple plank footbridge within the forest fringe. At the time of writing the continuing forest path is consumed by half-a-dozen windblown trees, a spot of ducking and weaving to the right soon restores progress within the narrow forest ride. Damp in places, advance to a tiny burn, draped by a few windfall firs, again avoid by dipping into the near canopy to the right. Re-emerging advance to a hand-gate in the forest bounding wall, the continuation of the wall dipping off the Roman Wall on Sewingshields Crags, heading north-westward on the alignment of the Black Dyke – no hint of brass bands – rather an ancient tribal boundary, while you may detect a slight rise to the wall the term 'dyke' meant wall.

15 The Ordnance Survey map gives sucker to the notion that a path leads on north-eastwards across the open wilderness of Haughton Common!. No chance! You'll probably be the second person on the footpath in the last decade – after the author. Being Access Land gives positive latitude for a spot of creative walking. Thatch Sike is no place for the unwebfooted.

Adding to the cautionary tale – the author encountered an adder basking on a slab of rock in this vicinity. So turn immediately right, descending replicate the actions of the local shepherd aboard his quad bike, simply ford Haughtongreen Burn. Notice the pile of stones close by, the remnants of a two-roomed shepherd's sheiling. Angle up half-left skirting the bracken onto the emerging scarp ridge. Pass a pair of rocks, that just might show evidence of Bronze Age cup-marking, though it is more likely to be purely natural etching. Gaining the brow of Crow Crags enjoy the path through

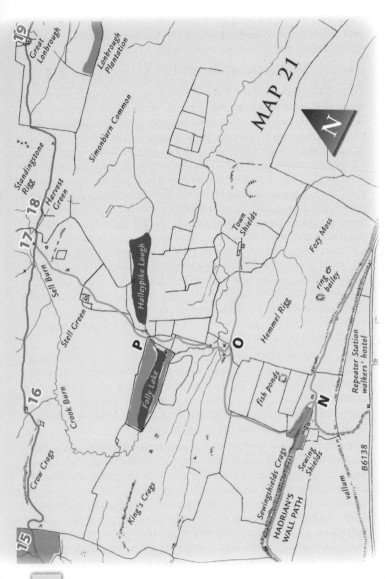

MAP 21

N

19

Great Lonbrough

Lonbrough Plantation

Sinonburn Common

Standingstone Rigg

Harvest Green

18

17

Sell Burn

Stell Green

Halleypike Lough

Town Shields

Fozy Moss

Hemmel Rigg

ring & bailey

P

O

Folly Lake

16

Crook Burn

fish ponds

N

Repeater Station walkers' hostel

Crow Crags

King's Crags

Sewingshields Crags

Sewing Shields

HADRIAN'S WALL PATH

vallum

B6138

15

the light bracken, created by cattle and sheep, with several good moments to pause and scan the rocky heather garden. Declining towards a massive sheepfold, the wing walls gave wind shelter whatever the prevailing storm, take leave of the remnant ridge. Go left, following the sheep in skipping over a feeder stream of Crook Burn. Ascend to the right of a bank of bracken onto the tree-crowned Harraway Hills knoll.

16 An important landmark, the trees have grown within an old sheepfold. A solitary weathered standing stone, the Harraway Stone, a few metres beyond, suggests that this hillock was significant to people living in this area several thousand years ago too. Next to it, a low tableau of rock makes a fine spot to picnic and ponder the location. The rising skyline of trees and rocks that is Sewingshields Crags seems remote to the south, beyond the heathery scarp edges of King's and Queen's Crags. Legend claims that King Arthur and his knights sleep in its craggy chest awaiting a fabled return.

Sheep certainly come to our rescue when it comes to navigation from here on, canny wee beasties, they live here and are as keen as any not to get wet feet. So take their lead in trending ENE off the low rigg. Latterly you'll notice some ragged order of stones betraying an old shieling and its near bounding walls. Bear off half-left just as these begin, faithful to our woolly guides. Keep an eye on the mid-distant scarp of The Lumps, our path aiming for its dip slope, the sheep path skips a handful of tiny burns. Passing a small patch of bracken notice evidence of a limestone sink, and then the small rectangular outline of a shieling, just like the one encountered upon emergence from Wark Forest. Over the brow to the south, the barns of Stell Green, a remote farmstead accessed by a lonely track from Sewingshields Farm. Now bear half-right over the burn, and along the south slope of The Lumps keeping below the bracken. The rank purple moor grass making progress less pleasant than heretofore. But the sight of a waymark post restores one's faith in the course of the footpath, if not the path.

17 A path linking to Stell Green is indicated right and therefore makes a line of connection with Hadrian's Wall via the interlaken track between the well-hidden and seldom visited Halleypike Lough and Folly Lake (see Stell Green Link on pages 125-126). Continue through a broken gate, hop over Sell Burn - sell

meant 'willow', not that there is any growing here today, the nearest being found on the carr, on the shores of Halleypike Lough. Rushes ease at the brow, passing the northern end of a delta-shaped bield wall onto the close-cropping sheep pasture of Harvest Green.

18 Follow on the northern edge of this most pleasant dry ridge, with the peaty mire of Standingstone Rigg immediately left. Cross evidence of old shallow quarrying to pass a waymark post at the junction of paths. Notice a circular sheepfold on the left brow beyond a brief marsh. Hold the sheepfold in your mind, as you advance with the green track, curving left to a gate in the enclosure wall.

At this point consider diverting back westwards onto the ridge towards the sheepfold. The attraction? The discovery of a line of ancient standing stones, origin of the ridge-name, seemingly defining a boundary as they continue down the slope in either direction.

Turning back to the footpath, go through the gate and follow the clear green track into the pasture field. Gradually drift left amid rushes and thistles to reach the nearest timber barn at Great Lonbrough. Locate a waymark post directing right, close round by the farmhouse garden wall. Notice the small stone privy over the first wall. Pass round to the left (south side) of the farmhouse, via a fence gate at the corner of the garden. Hugging the garden wall right, to reach a waymark post beside the timber barn on the west side of the buildings.

19 Continue south-westward through the nettles and rushes of the pasture field, latterly rising to a gate in the enclosure wall. Follow the green track, which veers left (south), then, once over the ford, west by a waymark post, upon the close-cropped turf of Standingstone Rigg. **18** Pass to the right of the bield wall at the western end of Harvest Green. Dipping into the rushes, ford Sell Burn and clamber over the broken gate in a fence. The imminent pasture is chocked with rank clumps of molinia, advance to, and beyond, the waymark post **17**; a path branches to Sewingshields via nearby Stell Green, however, there is little hint of the said path.

Keep intent on the south-west course, the one landmark, and destination, a clump of trees on Harraway Hills. Ford a small burn, rise to follow a sheep trod passing a patch of bracken aligned with a limestone sinks. Latterly the trod is lost in a mass of rushes. Ford another burn, the trod continues more certainly to the shallow ridge-end site of a shieling, towards the two pines and a birch set in the old sheepfold **16**. Bear down left fording the infant Crook Burn, clamber onto the shallow ridge beside a large sheepfold complex. Advancing along the gently rising ridge over Crow Crags, continue down with the quad track taking the easy line right, where a traverse quad track leads by a shieling ruin to ford Haughtongreen Burn. Stumble through the tough clumps of molinia to a wooden hand-gate left, gaining entry into Wark Forest **15**.

GREAT LONBROUGH TO CASTLE DENE   (**22**)
4 km | **2.5** miles > **1.6** hours

19 Coming round the garden wall go through the gate in the fence, join the track as it leaves the farmyard via a gate, the farm access track departs left. However, the footpath heads straight across the pasture due east to a gate, then on down a gentle ridge towards a circular sheepfold. Short of the sheepfold, drift down left to a culvert over Hopeshield Burn.

20 The dell is lightly sprinkled with alder trees, but no trace of a path to be seen. The footpath effectively rises, progressively up the slope, onto the ridge to a gate in a wall. The presence of

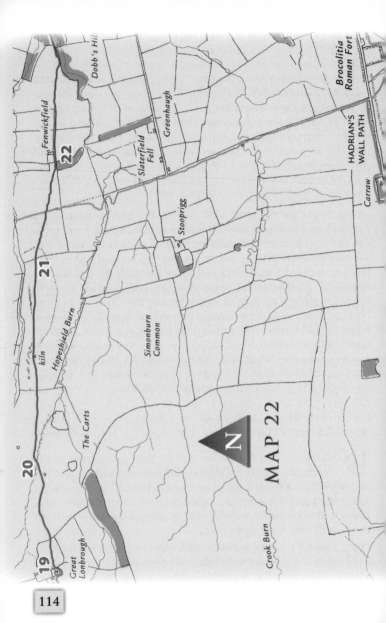

a natural drainage hollow, conventionally referred to as a sink, confirms a geological change to an underlying limestone. A clear green path strides on, to the right of a shallow limestone quarry, clearly of some age as it is totally turfed over, a protruding bank on the right containing the remains of a limekiln. Continue past a second shallow quarry. Ahead on the right, gracing the eastern skyline some five miles distant at Kirkeaton, are three wind turbines. While half-right, the somewhat closer skyline hilltop feature, Limestone Corner on Hadrian's Wall. The Moss Troopers' Trail meets the Wall some quarter-of-a-mile east of this brow.

21 On reaching a gate in a fence, the green track enters somewhat rougher cattle pasture, running on through the remains of a large walled boundary bank. Advancing across a second linear bank feature, cross a bridleway, continue towards the obvious barns of Fenwickfield (silent 'w'). Aim for a gate beside the conifer plantation, the northern shelter strip has recently been felled, and at the time of writing the trees have not been removed.

22 Pass on by the single-storey house, sporting a lovely garden, join the track. Follow this track via gates, down into the mature conifer dell of Castle Dene. Pass the sad ruins of Simonburn Castle, a pele tower with a notice warning visitors to be wary of crumbling masonry, the roadway is now concreted. The village name Simonburn actually derives from Simon's beorg, though the inference is not to this particular structure, rather to a grander place perhaps in the vicinity of Nunwick, the seat of the Allgood family – quite a claim to be all virtuous! The three great houses in this part of the North Tyne are Chipchase, Park End, and Nunwick (the latter famed for its exotic garden – only open to the public on one precious day each year).

CASTLE DENE TO GREAT LONBROUGH |>>

The track passes through gates en route to Fenwickfield, a delight-fully secluded cottage **22**. Pass to the left of the cottage, through a gate beside the conifer belt, the right-hand plantation has recently been felled. Slant half-right through the rushes, traverse the rough cattle pasture to a waymark post set upon a linear bank beside the line of a north/south aligned bridleway. Continue westward, with some evidence of a path through the pasture, slip through a further curved enclosure bank to a fence gate **21**. The sheep-cropped pasture has but thistles to hamper a flowing stride. Keep the shallow limestone quarrying to the right, pass a ruined limekiln to reach a gate in a wall by limestone sink hollows. Now on rougher pasture with no hint of a path, maintain the westward course, crossing dykes, dipping into the Hopeshield Burn valley. Traverse the second small culvert bridge **20** set below the circular sheepfold on the ridge to the left, just before the last clump of alders. Rise with the apparent path, notice the old rigg & furrow cultivation traces on the right of the ridgetop. Passing through a gate to reach the muddy access track at Great Lonbrough Farm.

CASTLE DENE TO NEWBROUGH (23)
7.7 km | 4.8 miles > **2.3** hours

23 Reaching a junction at the foot of dingles, pass the green letterbox and bear right over the bridge onto the tarmac of Castle Lane. This rural byway leads directly into the village of Simonburn. Notice the post office, immediately left, also serving as a tearoom and licensed B&B. Hereon the trail follows lovely country lanes. At the green make a point of glancing at the impressive parish church of St Mungo (also known as St Kentigern, This is no chapel of ease, the scale speaks of some considerable local importance. Indeed, there was a time when the church served the largest parish in England, stretching as far as the Scottish border.

24 Leave the green, continue by Redlion Cottages down to a minor junction, turn right crossing the road-bridge spanning Crook Burn. This is the same burn you crossed several miles ago on the landmark knoll of faraway Harraway Hill, shortly after leaving Wark Forest and clambering over Crow Crags. The road ascends to Hall Barns, where the more regular public road swings left.

25 Continue south, the road sign 'gates' indicates the peaceful nature of this country road. Keep left at the next turn, and after the right-hand bend pass through a sequence of three gates, climbing Ark Hill via Sharpley Farm, an equestrian centre offering tuition in carriage driving and conventional horse-craft: in 1797 the farm-name was recorded as 'Sheep lan'.

The views east across the North Tyne valley ensure a steady

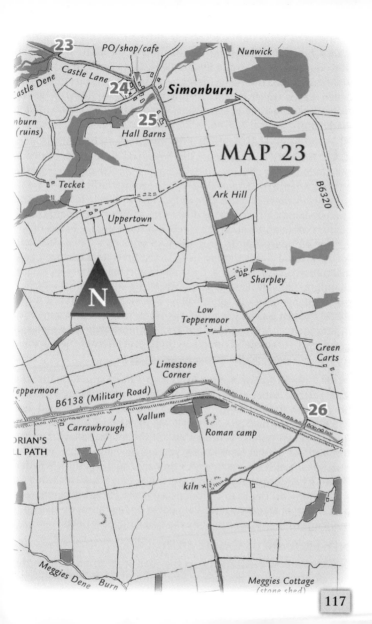

23

PO/shop/cafe

Nunwick

Castle Dene   Castle Lane

Castle Dene

24

Simonburn

nburn
(ruins)

25

Hall Barns

MAP 23

B6320

Tecket

Ark Hill

Uppertown

N

Sharpley

Low
Teppermoor

Green
Carts

Limestone
Corner

Teppermoor

B6138 (Military Road)

26

Vallum

Carrawbrough

Roman camp

DRIAN'S
LL PATH

kiln ×

Meggies Dene Burn

Meggies Cottage
(stone shed)

117

appreciative stride until, with almost disbelief, we arrive at Hadrian's Wall. A fine mural section of the monument, including the remains of turret 29a stands in the field at Black Carts Farm. In case you're wondering, the farm-name meant 'poor soil', to contrast the nearby Green Carts, which meant 'healthy soil'. Close scrutiny of an OS map above Greenlee Lough reveals a matching duo submerged in Wark Forest, grid ref 774715.

26 While the National Trail can be joined to east or west, the Moss Troopers' Trail continues journeying down to the South Tyne, the golden valley of many a moss trooper's roguish desire. Cross the Military Road, a main road alive with speeding traffic so 'tek care' as they say in these parts! A gate with a low step stile left, and large stone balking entry to 4x4 joy drivers, gains entry in to a large cattle pasture. Walking through the ditch and fragmentary banks of the vallum, aim part right to keep the new enclosure fence close left. As the ground swells slightly, keep to the brow, to a narrower gate inserted askew to the fence. Go through and follow the fence right, shielding a shallow limestone quarry. At the wall notice the double gothic arched limekiln right. Follow the wall down through three gates, the last a rickety wooden specimen with another large rock in attendance. A green lane ensues, leading down via a series of gates past Torneysfell Cottage, with its collection of memorabilia from a rural working life, join a surfaced road.

27 Refer to The Roman Ring map 12 on page 69. After the cottage notice the pent-roofed stone shed right, by a roofless bowed hut, the remnants of Meggie's Cottage, sadly reviled as a witch. However, her name lives on in 'Meggies Burn Dene', the stream flowing down from Coventina's Well at Brocolitia. Follow the road through the gate at Lane House, you are now level with, and only quarter-of-a mile distant from ('be prepared' for this), the site Baden Powell's first formal Boy Scout campsite at Carr Edge - recorded on s a monument. The road continues, en route for Newbrough, with a fine view of Meggies Dene. Pass down by Newborough Hall farm buildings to the village street by the Red Lion, how neat!

NEWBROUGH TO CASTLE DENE |>>

Set course from Newbrough up the road leading north from the Red Lion. Keep with the tarmac road through gates at Lane House and **27** Torneysfell Cottage, where you enter a green lane. Ignore the ladder-stile near the top, continue to the decrepit wooden gate with the boulder beyond. Ascend with the wall close left, via two further gates to reach a fence, note the pair of limekilns just ahead. Follow the fence right, shielding a shallow quarry, to reach a gate inserted askew to the fence. Go through and keep to the higher ground. Trending half-right to come alongside a new fence heading north-east. Pass throught the vallum ditch to a gate (stile on right) leading onto the Military Road. **26** Cross the busy B6318 with due care, to encounter Hadrian's Wall and the National Trail. Continue along the gated road, more popular with tractors and the odd cyclist than your average car, a blessing indeed. The road offers unrivalled views across the tree-dappled North Tyne valley, en route to the little estate village of Simonburn. Pass Hall Barns **25** descending to cross Crook Burn, then bear up left to the village green **24**, some two miles removed from the Roman Wall. Keep right of the church and left of the post office, pass into Castle Lane then head north-west. The tarmac ends as the lane dips into the wooded dingle **23**. Fork left, by the green letterbox, ascending the concrete roadway climb by the rubble ruins of Simonburn Castle.

LINK PATHS

(DESCRIBED NORTHBOUND ONLY)

The three east/west, or even west/east, linear paths are fine and dandy as they stand, forming the basis of The Roman Ring. However, within the Conservation Corridor five key north/south routes have been identified, enabling walkers to confidently plan ahead and customise their own expeditions. The single focus of the National Trail need never again frustrate visitors new to the area seeking to enjoy a few days 'on the Wall'. For you can revel in a far more fulfilling walking experience combining various elements of this historic landscape.

These north south routes are intended to be used as bridges between the Roman Ring to the south, the National Trail in the middle or the Moss Trooper's Trail in the north, to create shorter circular walks of only a few days duration for those who would like to see it in the round.

The northern march of the Pennine Way over Blenkinsopp Common makes a valuable contribution to The Roman Ring enabling walkers to create a fabulous three-day circular excursion in the western sector. Take the first third of the eastbound Roman Ring, this south-north bridge of the Pennine Way, and the westward part of the Wall back to Brampton, to give a fine exposé of some of Cumbria's 'lost country'. Forgive it its dampness, you'll appreciate a firm tread elsewhere all the more!

A Arriving at the intersection gate from the west (grid ref 658604), bear acutely left on a path through the pasture that makes a dive into a small re-entrant burn. One could imagine that heavily laden backpackers will have uttered a few irreverent words to the attendant Galloway cattle, standing here goggle-eyed at transient trekkers. The path reaches a gate at Ulpham, the name means 'owl's valley'. Keep left along the gated lane, bearing right at the gate enter a field to the right of Batey Shield. A shiel or shieling was 'a summer farmstead' too hostile and unproductive in winter for man or beast; the family and its animals would decamp in late spring, making use of the temporary abundance of the shiel while hay grew in the main meadows of the home farm. Descend the pasture to a footbridge and cross the road.

B From the facing gate follow the track to Greenriggs. Pass to the left of the hippy house via stiles to head straight up a pasture to a ladder-stile in a fence. Now entering Access Land; the path marches on, do not be lured by the more obvious quad bike track, swing only gently left. Keeping to the higher, drier ground aim for a waymark post beside a new fence aligned north/south.

C Within a few metres the fence becomes less pristine, but no less tight. The path next traverses a hollow that, from a distance, would suggest damp going, close acquaintance does nothing to dispel the aforethought. A few duckboards wouldn't go amiss! Advance to the footbridge at the far end, constructed from an old beam. A rise, then another shallow damp hollow on Galloping Rigg leads to a ladder-stile, which has duckboarding. Stride on, glancing by the fence corner near Eadleystone, the shepherd's cot ruin, head on over Blenkinsopp Common – this place-name would appear

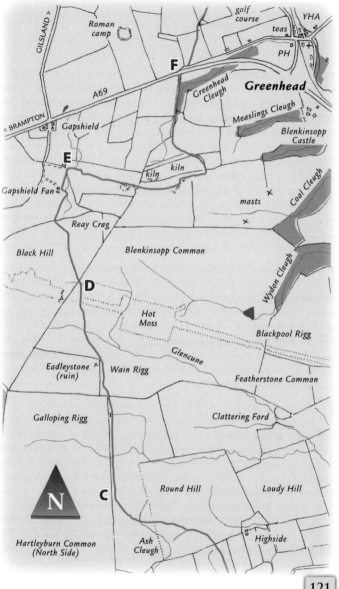

to be tautological, combining the Welsh blaen 'valley head' with the Old English hope 'a valley'. Advance on a discernible path through the heather to the ladder-stile.

D A brief detour to the lonesome Ordnance Survey column, beside a low stone wall quarried scarp, provides a moment to look at one intriguing feature. Looking south-east along the plateau top you'll detect a change in the vegetation, this broad belt was the result of the wartime creation of a mock airfield and runway, aimed at deceiving German bombers. Continue north over the plateau of Black Hill, place-names with 'black' invariably an indicator of peat. After rain you'll know just what it is like to walk on water! Directly ahead across the valley, backed by the far-flung forestry of Spadeadam, is a large square building, Gilsland Spa Hotel. Descend to a stile, passing down by the pond and derelict buildings, former brick offices associated with Gap Shields colliery. Join the subsequent short causeway to reach a felt-clad hideaway.

E Go through the adjacent gate and follow the open track east, this was once a railway conveying coal from the colliery down to Blenkinsopp. Passing under the pylon line, spot a limekiln left. Advance to a ladder-stile, and beyond a small ruin, a further ladder-stile. The greenway – currently lined by round rush bales – soon weaves through an old limestone quarry to a stile left. Follow the track to a further stile, head straight on, under pylon lines, once more following the track via gates, beside beech and coppice woodland to meet the A69.

F Choose when to cross wisely: The Pennine Way climbing steps to stiles on the far side, some thirty metres to the right. Angle half-right across the field to a ladder-stile, briefly entering Access Land. The next ladder-stile puts the path beside a wall and pine copse adjacent to Haltwhistle Golf Course. At the next ladder-stile our path comes into immediate contact with the Roman Wall Vallum. Cross and follow these rough banks along the edge of the course (noting the clubhouse, situated down to the left, a welcome port of call for walkers' refreshment). Soon Thirlwall Castle comes into view, the path slips down the bank from a mass of gorse. At the ladder-stile step onto the road beside the English Heritage car park, meeting up with Hadrian's Wall Path.

This route connects all three components of Hadrian's Wall Conservation Corridor, opening up several attractive grand circular expeditions of two/three days duration to east and west.

34 Simply follow on up the valley from the foot of the Herding Hill steps, delving into its wooded craggy depths. Haltwhistle townsfolk have long adored this stroll, the gradient gentle all the way. This was the scene of considerable industrial activity down the years, with coal, fire clay, and lime, hauled down the valley on a narrow-gauge railway. The path follows the track bed of the railway, which ran from south Cawfields quarry following the Haltwhistle Burn (the re-named Caw Burn), past the fort overlooking New Bridge, and adjacent to the Milecastle Inn, over the Military Road, then down to the main line at Haltwhistle. Notice the elegantly restored chimney, a remnant of the South Tyne Colliery, and higher, two sets of collapsed lime kilns. The Romans will most certainly have exploited its bounty of stone and coal. Footbridges aid progress via hand-gates eventually rising to join the Military Road.

G Cross cautiously, the traffic tends to come helter-skelter! Follow the verge on the north side to where the road is carried over Haltwhistle Burn upon an embankment. Bear left, down beside the embankment wall, cross the bridge culvert to a ladder-stile. This was the old level of the road, with the railway on a level crossing. Continue on upstream, keep to the green causeway to a stile onto the road: Roman marching camps are associated with the invisible course of the Stanegate. At this point meet up with the Pennine Way and Hadrian's Wall Path emerging from Cawfields Quarry.

H The Moss Troopers' Trail connection continues along the road via the cattle-grid and on past Cawfields Farm, where the road becomes a track leading to East Cawfields. Advance to a gate to the right, traverse a field to a footbridge spanning Caw Burn. Pass to the left of the newly refurbished Low Close a'Burns rising to a ladder-stile. Waymarking guides the re-routed footpath left of the young coppice at High Close a'Burns, bear right to a gate above the house. Turn left, a waymark post lurking in the rushes guides diagonally north, by a wall corner to a stile over the roadside wall at Ventners Hall, continuing north to Edges Green.

The Pennine Way's southern approach to the Wall provided the potential for a western circuit, this link uses its northward escape from the Wall to fashion 'the perfect three-day round' in the eastern sector of the Conservation Corridor. Tourist advice frequently suggests Bardon Mill Station as the smart point to access to the popular Whin Sill section of the Roman Wall from the Newcastle/ Carlisle Railway. This is made all the more credible with this link through to Wark Forest via Thorngrafton Common and Rapishaw Gap. However, check rail timetables carefully; not all trains stop at Bardon Mill.

I From the station wander up into the village, scene of annual conker championships, where winners receive tankards inscribed 'We came, we saw, we conkered'. The village shop offers scope to stock up for the day ahead, Bowes Hotel fayre may tend to slow you down, while Errington Reay's beautiful pots over the way, will burden you utterly (come back on another day and acquire one or two, they are superb for practical home use and garden ornament). Follow the village street right, at the war memorial turning left up the road running under the A69. At the first junction opt to follow the road right, climbing by Hott, a lone cottage. Folk who warm to landscape symbolism will be intrigued by the term 'hott', for it indicates the site of a lost ring of trees.

J At the small green triangle at the top, bear left to West End Town. Before the farm, a bridleway sign directs right, up a green lane. Keep within the lane to a ladder-stile and gate, the lane then funnels out onto Thorngrafton Common. Trace a diminishing path up through the bracken and heather (which is absolutely gorgeous in August), rising to a broad gap in the ridge-top wall: the meeting with The Roman Ring which bears right, to the Ordnance Survey column on the Roman signal station surmounting Barcombe.

41 The link follows the Ring down the footpath due north to the stile onto the road – crossing Stanegate at this point. Continue down the road past the impressive Crinkedykes limekiln, notice the orange stain on the tarmac issuing from mine drainage. Follow the road up to the Military Road, bear right some 50 metres and cross the road to a recessed stile.

K A greenway leads into the dip, crosses the Vallum, then angles right, over the end of a strip lynchet terrace to a ladder-stile. Turn left in front of the prominent limekiln, swinging up right en route to Rapishaw Gap.

L Hadrian's Wall and the Pennine Way National Trails meet and part at this point. Join The Pennine Way as it leaves the Wall via the ladder-stile. The path continues, bearing half-right across the marshy hollow, rising to a ladder-stile and sheepfold, (the left-hand path goes to a pair of limekilns (proving that limestone, sandwiches the Whin Sill). The path heads north. At the next ladder-stile enter Access Land, the farmer is participating in the National Park Authority Drovers' Project – encouraging the traditional Blue Grey, and Galloway cattle breeds grazing of this land, to help control the rank growth of moorland grass species. The path traverses Jenkins Burn, the outflow of Broomlee Lough, then winds round a heather rigg to cross the over the next scarp with its double fences denying access onto the farmland of West and East Hotbank.

M Before descending the scarp on the greenway, make the briefest of detours along the north side of the fold wall some 50 metres, to locate the so-called Sacrifice Stone, a rock table with a sculpted bowl of unknown age. Backtrack, follow the Pennine Way down the Cragend bank, across the moor pasture, drained by the headstreams of Greenlee Lough to marry with the Moss Troopers' Trail over a ladder-stile, upon the track east of East Stonefolds, leading into Wark Forest.

STELL GREEN LINK – SEE MAP ON PAGE 110

At the eastern end of the Whin Sill scarp there is just one scenic connection linking the National Trail with the Moss Troopers' Trail.

N Immediately east of Sewingshields Wood, an open track leads north from a bungalow slipping back under the wooded scarp to cross a cattle-grid. At the next grid, entering Access Land, stay with the open track which bears right as the principal access to Town Shields Farm.

O Approaching the next gate bear left, as intimated by the footpath waymark post, slanting down the bank and by a pair of tall gothic-arched limekilns. Approaching a broad ford step left over the plank bridge. The track leads on to a gate in a fence exiting Access Land, and rises over a pasture brow with a fine view west over Folly Lake (private fishing). Note the pair of upturned aircraft wheels lurking in the plantation close left as the track dips over the burn linking from Halleypike Lough. Advance to the next gate, re-entering Access Land, keep with the track north. Halleypike Lough may seem a bleak sheet of water but ducks and swans in abundance seem to find it attractive.

P The green track (below) leads up to the lone cottage of Stell Green. Waymarking guiding right of the buildings, to a stile in a fence, to embark upon moorland pasture. Traverse the marshy ground to a waymark post on the rising ground, glancing over the left-hand shoulder of the knoll – thus both avoiding the ruined enclosure on the top and the bare peat-bouldered northern slope. Cross the succeeding marshy hollow, stepping over Crook Burn to reach a solitary waymark post thus joining the Moss Troopers' Trail, to all intents in the middle of nowhere. The key landmarks from this point on the Trail are the bield wall on the near ridge-top of Harvest Green, accessed due east via a decrepit fence gate, and the clump of trees on Harraway Hills, half-a-mile to the south-west across the apparently featureless, rushy pasture.

Stell Green

So you fell asleep and didn't get off the westbound train at Hexham, or the eastbound train at Bardon Mill, despair not, Haydon Bridge station comes to your rescue with a lovely link route onto The Roman Ring. Actually, this large Tynedale village is a splendid springboard being well served by shops, inns and public transport connections.

Q Walk over the level-crossing, embarking on North Bank pass the handsome Congregational Church. After some 100 metres find a tarmaced roadway right, signed St John's Catholic Church and Presbytery. Follow this access road uphill, glance right to see the church, dedicated to St John of Beverley, before crossing the ladder-stile with its lever bar. Pass through the small pony paddock to a metal hand-gate, and up the bank ahead to a kissing-gate. Continue, now in pasture with the hedge close left, via a further kissing-gate to a hand-gate onto the minor road at the top facing The Tofts.

R The view back over Tynedale is pleasing, revealing both valley and village. Turn right, follow the narrow road passing a metal seat, one suspects that it reflects the climate, chilly on the cheeks when cold, boiling to the bot when hot! Keep to the road as it bends left ignoring the footpath off right, rising by the Old Church; built c.1190 from Roman camp stone, restored in 1882. A moment's aside is rewarded with an intimate view upon a charming little church and tree-sheltered kirkyard, the yew-lined path quite Transylvanian. Though kept locked, the church contains a Roman altar font. The church lay in the midst of the medieval village of Haydon, meaning 'hay hill'. The arrival of the railway the last nail in the coffin for this tiny community, born again as a significant township in the valley, either side of the South Tyne, hence the name Haydon Bridge.

Follow the winding lane crossing Cruel Sike; an old couplet hints to the traumatic Border Reiving origins of this stream-name:

> *"Till the cruel Syke wi' Scottish blode rins red*
> *Thoo mauna sowe corn by Tyneside".*

Arriving at West and East Haydon Farms bear left and take the left fork, long vehicle or not! Ascend by the shelterbelt eventually reaching a small green triangle thus meeting The Roman Ring at its entry into Fell Lane from the New Alston road. *BON VOYAGE*

MAP INDEX